How to use

Issue 98

The 91 daily readings in this issue of *Explore* are designed to help you understand and apply the Bible as you read it each day.

It's serious!

We suggest that you allow 15 minutes each day to work through the Bible passage with the notes. It should be a meal, not a snack! Readings from other parts of the Bible can throw valuable light on the study passage. These cross-references can be skipped if you are already feeling full up, but will expand your grasp of the Bible. *Explore* uses the NIV2011 Bible translation, but you can also use it with the NIV1984 or ESV translations.

Sometimes a prayer box will encourage you to stop and pray through the lessons—but it is always important to allow time to pray for God's Spirit to bring his word to life, and to shape the way we think and live through it.

We're serious!

All of us who work on *Explore* share a passion for getting the Bible into people's lives. We fiercely hold to the Bible as God's word—to honour and follow, not to explain away.

1 Find a time you can read the Bible each day

2 Find a place where you can be quiet and think

3 Ask God to help you understand

4 Carefully read through the Bible passage for today

5 Study the verses with Explore, taking time to think

6 Pray about what you have read

thegoodbook
COMPANY

Opening up the Bible

Welcome to Explore

Being a Christian isn't a skill you learn, like carpentry or flower arranging. Nor is it a lifestyle choice, like the kind of clothes you wear, or the people you choose to hang out with. It's about having a real relationship with the living God through his Son, Jesus Christ. The Bible tells us that this relationship is like a marriage.

It's important to start with this, because many Christians view the practice of daily Bible reading as a Christian duty, or a hard discipline that is just one more thing to get done in our busy, modern lives.

But the Bible is God speaking to us: opening his mind to us on how he thinks, what he wants for us and what his plans are for the world. And most importantly, it tells us what he has done for us in sending his Son, Jesus Christ, into the world. It's the way the Spirit shows Jesus to us, and changes us as we behold his glory.

The Bible is not a manual. It's a love letter. And as with any love letter, we'll want to treasure it, and make time to read and re-read it, so we know we are loved, and discover how we can please the one who loves us. Here are a few suggestions for making your daily time with God more of a joy than a burden:

💙 *Time:* Find a time when you will not be disturbed and when the cobwebs are cleared from your mind. Many people have found that the morning is the best time as it sets you up for the day. If you're not a "morning person", then last thing at night or a mid-morning break might suit you. Whatever works for you is right for you.

💙 *Place:* Jesus says that we are not to make a great show of our religion *(see Matthew 6:5-6)*, but rather, to pray with the door to our room shut. Some people plan to get to work a few minutes earlier and get their Bible out in an office or some other quiet corner.

💙 *Prayer:* Although *Explore* helps with specific prayer ideas from the passage, try to develop your own lists to pray through. Use the flap inside the back cover to help with this. And allow what you read in the Scriptures to shape what you pray for yourself, the world and others.

💙 *Share:* As the saying goes: *expression deepens impression.* So try to cultivate the habit of sharing with others what you have learned. Why not join our Facebook group to share your encouragements, questions and prayer requests? Search for *Explore: For your daily walk with God.*

And remember, *it's quality, not quantity, that counts:* better to think briefly about a single verse than to skim through pages without absorbing anything, because it's about developing your relationship with the living God. The sign that your daily time with God is real is when you start to love him more and serve him more wholeheartedly.

Tim Thornborough
Editor

Jesus' supper

As Easter approaches, we're going to track through Matthew's account of the Passion, starting with the farewell supper party he held for his friends.

Jesus' final supper party with his friends is, in the end, ruined by Judas, but it is not a failure. Jesus gives us something extremely precious to remember him by; something simple but profound; something they ate then, but which would continue until Jesus comes again.

Bread and wine

Read Matthew 26:26-30

There was nothing different about the bread and wine. It is the meaning that Jesus attaches to the supper which makes it so special.

❷ *What was he really saying as he gave them the bread and wine to eat?*

This is for you! My sufferings tomorrow are for you; my broken body, my poured-out blood for your sins.

Looking back

This was a priceless farewell gift. But it wasn't just for that occasion. It was Jesus' intention that his followers would celebrate this meal over and over again, and be reminded of his sacrificial death. The early church made the breaking of bread a central part of their practice (see Acts 2:42).

❷ *Do you value Jesus' supper as you should? Are you glad to meet at his table to remember his priceless gift to you?*
❷ *Or has it become routine and dry?*

The bread—to remind believers that his body was broken for them. The wine—to remind believers of his blood shed for them, as a pledge of forgiveness.

Looking around

The Lord's Supper encourages us to realise that we are part of Jesus' family—a redeemed community with a task to do. It's why taking communion alone is missing a big part of the picture.

Looking ahead

Re-read Matthew 26:29-30

❷ *What do you think Jesus means here?*

The feast is for remembering; but also for looking forward to when Jesus shall feast once again with all his disciples.

☑ Apply

❷ *When was the last time you took part in the Lord's Supper?*
❷ *Which aspect of its meaning do you most focus on?*
❷ *How can you grow to appreciate the other two dimensions?*

⌃ Pray

Thank God for this precious reminder, and give thanks for all that it means.

"I'd never do that"

"I'd never do a thing like that!" And yet haven't we all been shocked and ashamed at the way we have behaved, or thought?

Never!
Read Matthew 26:31-33

❓ *Why is what Jesus says in verse 31 so shocking after what has just happened?*
❓ *What is the nature of the promise in verse 32?*
❓ *How does Peter react?*

Peter knew just what Jesus was saying; and he was filled with horror and indignation at the prediction. How could Jesus think they would desert their Shepherd when his enemies came to take him? Never!

But Jesus knows his sheep. He is not surprised at our weakness. He realises just how capable we are of total failure, unless he keeps us from it. Yes, Peter did love Jesus. And the last thing he wanted to do was to betray him. But emotions are changeable, and Peter hadn't reckoned on being gripped with fear. He had thought his love would stand any test.

Peter was capable of far worse than he had ever imagined—for not only would he run from his Lord with the others, but also...

You will deny me!
Read Matthew 26:34-35

❓ *What makes Peter and the rest of the disciples so confident, do you think?*
❓ *Do you think you would have been any different in the same situation?*

Jesus couldn't have put it more clearly. It certainly ought to have made Peter think. Hadn't Jesus always been right before? Hadn't he shown that he knew Peter better than Peter knew himself? Not even one of the disciples believed Jesus. None of them pleaded with God to prevent them failing in such a shameful way. None of them knew much at all of the evil lurking in their hearts.

⌄ Apply

❓ *Do you have an inflated view of your own steadfastness and ability to resist temptation?*
❓ *In what circumstances do you think you might be especially vulnerable to denying Christ? Or perhaps, just staying quiet and keeping your faith under the radar?*

TIME OUT

Read 1 Corinthians 10:1-14

Despite so many special blessings, notice the unthinkable sins that Israel fell into. We are no safer than Peter—unless we learn those lessons and depend on Christ's ability to keep us, not our own.

⌃ Pray

Pray the words of **Galatians 6:1-2** for others you know, and for yourself.

Man of sorrows

When it comes to the crunch, the most devoted of Jesus' followers are desperately weak and vulnerable. Which is why we need a Saviour who will stand for us...

Cup of horror
Read Matthew 26:36-39

- ❓ *What do you find surprising, or shocking about these verses?*
- ❓ *What is the "cup" that he fears to drink from (v 39)?*
- ❓ *What do the emotions expressed in these verses tell us about the cross?*
- ❓ *What do they tell us about the Lord?*

Just ahead of him was a prospect of appalling horror. This man, untainted by the sin all around him, was about to take all sin's evil upon himself. We cannot begin to get hold of the intensity of sorrow, the agony of his soul, which that prospect brought. We have only the faintest idea of the ugliness and terror of sin—but Jesus saw evil in its naked vileness, with the pure eyes of perfect holiness. Not for nothing was he called "the man of sorrows".

Now the "cup" containing all that foulness was in front of him, as if it were touching his lips. It was full of the most disgusting bitter poison, which he had to drink to the very bottom. It was filled with:

- **sin**: he was sinless, but he was determined to carry his people's sin.
- **guilt**: he was innocent, yet he had to bear his people's guilt.
- **wrath**: he was a delight to his Father, yet he had to bear the penalty of his people's sin and face his Father's wrath.

But as you will
Re-read Matthew 26:39

- ❓ *Was Jesus really turning his back on the work he had come to do?*
- ❓ *How does Jesus' prayer show what genuine prayer must look like?*

The pain seems unbearable, the cup seems undrinkable; the Son cries out in anguished revulsion—but then says, "If it is possible..." There was no other way. He knew that. He then says, "But as you will". Jesus' desire had not changed. It was still to do his Father's will. And the Lord Jesus didn't do it grudgingly. He was gladly willing. The horror is unthinkable, but he was ready to grasp the cup in both hands and drain it to its bitter bottom, so that there would be not one drop left for his people to bear.

🔺 Pray

Grieve over the sin which caused him infinite sorrow in order to save you from endless sorrow.

And praise him with all your heart that he has taken every drop himself.

Prepare for prayer

Time was fast moving on that emotion-filled night. Very soon they would be facing danger and separation. So what is Jesus' priority for his disciples?

When in doubt...

Read Matthew 26:40-44

❓ *How does Jesus want his disciples to be spending their time on the eve of Good Friday?*

❓ *What do they do instead?*

❓ *How is Jesus' statement at the end of verse 41 so insightful about us?*

Jesus leaves them very clear instructions as to how they need to spend this time (v 41). And yet they sleep on. Not that they were being lazy. It was late in the evening after a tremendously stressful day, and a big dinner with wine. Perhaps too the thought of being separated from Jesus was more than they could bear (see Luke 22:45).

Jesus knew all that. But he also knew that they had a deeper need than sleep. Think of their confident claims—sure, they would stick with their Lord. Here he is in his hour of greatest need—and here they are not even able to stay awake with him! Unless they wake up, unless they prepare with prayer, they will not be ready.

Too late

Read Matthew 26:45-46

❓ *How does Jesus react to the impending arrival of his betrayer?*

❓ *Why is he successful, when the disciples have failed?*

It is too late now for the disciples to prepare with prayer. The enemy is coming. Coming against Jesus and his followers; coming to arrest him; coming to crucify him. Perhaps the disciples would have preferred to hide or run away. But not Jesus. He stands tall and waits for the preordained story to play itself out.

✔ Apply

Jesus was ready to meet his enemies, ready to do his Father's will, ready to suffer indescribable shame and pain, because—*Jesus had made prayerful preparation*

We may not know what's about to face us; or we may be aware of great difficulties ahead. Either way, there is danger (v 41).

❓ *Are you being careless—or have you prepared with prayer?*

❓ *Are you "watching" to see potential dangers? Not so that you can run from them, but so that you can prayerfully prepare for them.*

We're often shocked by events, such as sudden illness, the death of a family member, the breakdown of a relationship, or the falling into sin of a friend or prominent Christian. Our bewilderment leaves us vulnerable to attack. We need to talk to the Lord about all these things before they happen, if we want to react in a godly way when they do.

❓ *How will you pray this through today?*

As a lamb…

The eleven may have let their Lord down, but they hadn't changed sides.

Jesus' "friend"
Read Matthew 26:47-50

❓ *Try to paint the scene in your imagination. What are the various characters feeling at this moment?*

❓ *What is so brutal about the sign Judas chose to identify Jesus?*

❓ *What do you think Jesus means in verse 50?*

A kiss is a greeting for a friend. And Jesus had certainly been a great friend to Judas. Although he knows it is a kiss of death, Jesus amazingly is still extending friendship (and forgiveness?) towards Judas.

Who's scared now?
Read Matthew 26:51-56

❓ *Why had they not arrested him before?*

❓ *How does Jesus react to the violence?*

He had never hidden from them. They could have attempted to take him any day as he taught in the temple—if they hadn't been afraid of the crowds. But they had no valid charge against him. So to avoid public uproar the arrest had to be in secret, at night. And because they feared Jesus, this unruly mob had been hired.

❓ *But look at the verses again. Who is obviously in control of the situation?*

All the armies of the world would never have been able to touch Jesus without his permission (v 53)! These violent men needed his permission to lay their hands on him and lead him away. And the one piece of resistance the disciples did offer was immediately dealt with by the captive himself!

So why was it such an undramatic event? Because Jesus was ready. He had no desire to resist his Father's will! His great concern was that the "Scriptures be fulfilled", as they declare the great plan of salvation.

⌄ Apply

Are you someone who is known as a friend of Jesus? Never deal Jesus a deadly kiss by pretending you are otherwise. I can remember hearing those condemning words: "But I thought you were a Christian…?" I don't want to hear them again. I want to honour Jesus always as my friend.

⌃ Pray

Ask God to strengthen those who face genuine hostility for their faith. Pray that they would not resort to violence, but would entrust themselves to the Lord.

And pray for yourself, that you would stand with our courageous brothers and sisters around the world and not be like verse 56 when opposition arrives.

No charge

The chief priests had acted decisively. Now, having arrested him, you can imagine their frustration—there were no charges to bring against him that stuck.

Somehow, before the night was out, they had to convince the Roman governor that this man deserved death...

Any evidence will do

Read Matthew 26:57-61

❓ *What do they attempt to do?*
❓ *Why does it fail?*
❓ *What is the charge that succeeds?*

They had to get evidence quickly. But how? Normally, giving false evidence was itself a crime worthy of death—but not tonight. Many were willing to try their hands at accusing the innocent Jesus; but, incredibly, they could find no two who had got their act together.

At last it looked as if they had success (v 61). Yet what a weak charge. Even if it had been true, it was hardly worthy of the death penalty. Surely not enough to impress Pilate, the governor.

TIME OUT

Read Hebrews 7:26; 9:14; 1 Peter 2:22

What a witness to Jesus' innocence! We find no one even pretending to have a real charge against him. There is no mention of Judas, who had lived for years close to Jesus, coming up with anything at all to accuse him of. And then even liars could find nothing to condemn him. He was perfectly sinless, and so could be a perfect Saviour.

Who will testify for him?

❓ *Where were most of the disciples all this time (see Matthew 26:58)?*

Would they be there declaring the holiness, the innocence, of their Master? And what of Peter? Would he be standing up for the Lord in line with his fearless boasts?

⌄ Apply

We should be slow to criticise the disciples for their weakness. Do we do any better, when there's probably no more danger than that of putting our own popularity at risk?

❓ *What would it look like to protest the purity, the worth, the holiness of the Saviour when his name is scorned or his honour attacked?*

⌃ Pray

Pray especially for those brothers and sisters who work in harsh, godless environments. Ask the Lord to help them work out how to be upright and friendly, without appearing to be joyless or judgmental.

And pray that you would be ready to speak a word in season and out of season in praise of our perfect Saviour.

Condemned

Frustrated by the dismal failure of the false witnesses, Caiaphas makes a desperate bid to trap Jesus into saying anything which might give him grounds for a valid charge.

Speak will you!

Read Matthew 26:62

Jesus had no need to say anything, no need to defend himself. His innocence was already painfully obvious to the high priest. Caiaphas was desperate; he had one last trump card to use to force Jesus to speak. Would Jesus answer when put under solemn oath to God?

Blasphemy?

Read Matthew 26:63-66

❓ *What is the High Priest asking—and how does he ask it?*
❓ *What do you make of Jesus' reply?*
❓ *Why does Caiaphas tear his robes?*

You can feel the frustration in his voice, but it has the desired effect. Jesus had willingly admitted to a "crime" worthy of death. It's as if Jesus is saying: "You know full well I am innocent of all other charges, but I gladly confess to being the Christ, the Son of God".

The tearing of his robes, supposedly a sign of distress, was perhaps merely to hide Caiaphas' relief and excitement at what Jesus had said. Blasphemy was the charge. And for anyone else it would certainly have been true. But their intense hatred blinded the accusers to the obvious truth.

Who's on trial here?

Read Matthew 26:67-68

❓ *Who are the death-deserving criminals here?*

···· **TIME OUT** ··································

Think carefully about Isaiah 50:5-9; 53:4; and Micah 5:1b.

❓ *What prophecies are being fulfilled?*

··

These men will meet Jesus again. He warns them of that in Matthew 26:64. Yes, it is he who is the mighty Christ, the Son of Man who will come in judgment and reign in glory. (They would have recognised Jesus' claims from Daniel 7:13-14.) Then they will be quite sure that he is innocent—and they are guilty.

🔼 Pray

We should feel compassion towards those who reject Christ, mock him and disdain his people. There is a judgment coming when all their mockery will ring hollow, and when his faithful people will be vindicated. What a terrible day that will be for them.

Pray that the Lord would have mercy on them before it is too late.

More sorrow

The scene changes for a while, moving away from Jesus' suffering—or does it?

But you, Peter!
Read Matthew 26:69-75

❷ *Do you empathise with Peter here?*

❷ *What do you think motivates him to deny Christ three times?*

❷ *How does verse 74 add to the picture of what was going on in Peter's heart and mind at this moment?*

The actions of the chief priests—their hatred, their contempt, their abuse of Jesus— were hard to bear. The violence of others, who joined in for no particular reason, added to that pain. The awful actions of Judas, in betraying not only a friend but someone who had shown him such love, was more than enough to break a sensitive heart like Jesus'. But here was someone who really did love Jesus, who had been closer than almost any other person, someone whom Jesus had chosen to be a key figure in his church, for whom Jesus was at this moment suffering, and for whose sins he was about to die...

❷ *So how do you think Jesus felt as he watched his friend Peter cursing and denying him?*

⌄ Apply

❷ *Have you ever denied that you have anything to do with him, or have you ever attempted to hide your love for him?*

❷ *Why, specifically, would your denial of Jesus be a deep cause of grief to him?*

But at least Peter was there! Notice that none of the other disciples were in any position to deny Jesus—they were nowhere to be seen! Their love for their Lord had not brought them into a vulnerable and possibly dangerous position; their love had not forced them to see what would happen to him.

❷ *Are you prepared to place yourself in a vulnerable position, even if you are unsure that you will stand the test?*

❷ *And do you have very real love for Jesus, like Peter—even if you often fail so miserably, and dishonour your Lord in your weakness?*

It was Peter, not the others, who fell so terribly. But it was Peter who was lovingly restored by his Lord; it was Peter who was specially commissioned to care for Christ's church; it was Peter who was so greatly used in his kingdom...

❷ *Is this relevant to you?*

Don't despair, instead...

Read John 21:7, 15-19; Acts 2:14, 37-41.

⌃ Pray

Talk to the Lord about past failures, and ask him for boldness to put yourself in places where you can show your love for him.

And pray for the divine strength you will need to be faithful under pressure.

No repentance, no faith

The tragedy of Judas's betrayal leads onto perhaps a greater tragedy as the full impact of what he has done strikes home. It is a bitter, heartbreaking story.

Led out bound

Read Matthew 27:1-2

As the servants and others (including Peter) waited in the courtyard of the high priest's palace, there must have been great tension and excitement. What would be the outcome of these extraordinary events?

Would this bizarre mock trial find enough "evidence" to condemn Jesus to death? At last the verdict had been reached. Now everyone would know, as Jesus is led out, bound.

Remorse…

Read Matthew 27:3-10

❷ *Judas too had been waiting—what was his reaction to the news?*
❷ *What does he do about it?*
❷ *Why do you think he hangs himself? What might be going on in his anguished mind at that moment?*

The deed had been done. For Judas there was no escape from its consequences. There is a terrible and tragic finality about the account. We would have liked a happy ending to the story, but there's nothing to take comfort in, except, once again, the testimony to the innocence of the Saviour. We would have pleaded with Judas, even after such a foul deed, to repent of his sin and to throw himself on the mercy of the one

who was about to die for sinners like him. We would have told him that there was no sin that was unforgivable, other than a final rejection of the Saviour.

… but no repentance

Re-read Matthew 27:3-5

❷ *How does Judas try to deal with his guilt?*
❷ *Why is this short-sighted?*

There was an unbearable sense of guilt, deep remorse, regret that he had ever brought such pain on himself—but no real repentance, no sorrow that he had sinned against Jesus, against God. And no repentance means no hope. Perhaps he hoped the chief priests could sort out his guilt, but there was no relief there either. Judas had lost faith in himself, but had not gained faith in the Saviour. His only hope was in death. But that would give him no ultimate relief, as he plunged into a lost eternity.

⌄ Apply

Guilt, sorrow and despair are never enough to save anyone. If that is all you have, then you are in a perilous position—learn from Judas's tragic end. Repentance, faith and love towards the Saviour are our desperate needs. Whatever your sin, turn to the only Saviour and live.

The God of all

When ancient armies went to war, they often carried their "gods" with them. Israel sometimes took the ark of the covenant into battle.

It's likely that this psalm was written as a song to be sung when the ark was brought back into Jerusalem after battle.

God of the planet
Read Psalm 24:1-2

> ❷ *What is David's staggering claim (v 1)?*
> ❷ *On what basis does he make it?*

The opening verses take us back to the opening of the Bible. This is no local or household god—one among the many of the nations of the earth. No, this is the God whose word banished darkness; the God who spoke, and brought order out of chaos.

Militant Islam and Hinduism continue to flourish, but Christianity is not in a competition with other faiths. We believe that the God of Abraham, Isaac and Jacob— the God and Father of our Lord Jesus Christ—is the one true and living God. All others are idols, impostors or worse. Such knowledge should not make us smug or arrogant; instead it should humble us that we've been chosen, and make us determined to humbly take the truth to others.

God of holiness
Read Psalm 24:3-6

> ❷ *Who is worthy to enter God's presence?*
> ❷ *What must they also do (v 6)? Why?*

David reprises his thoughts from Psalm 15: true worshippers know that what they bring in their hands is irrelevant to the God of heaven—he is concerned with what is inside them—whether they are "clean" from evil deeds. And not just our hands, but our hearts and lips also.

But Psalm 24:6 makes it clear that this kind of holiness is not something that we can pursue in isolation—as though rigorous discipline and determination can produce perfection. No, it can only be found in those who seek the face of God—who enter into a relationship with their holy creator God. We see here the unanswered question at the heart of Old Testament Israel—the question that only Jesus and his death for us can answer: *how can a sinner be put right with God?*

God of glory
Read Psalm 24:7-10

Those who carry the ark cry out to the gatekeepers, and the gatekeepers call back.

> ❷ *What is the conversation they have?*
> ❷ *What aspect of God's character do they emphasise here? Why?*

Spend some time in awe before God your Creator, who loves goodness and truth; hates falsehood and idols; and who bestows on you the holiness of Christ so that you are clean before him.

Coward's way out

Pilate had an eye to what those Jewish leaders could do to his career, but hadn't the guts to set the innocent man free. But maybe the crowds would let him off the hook?

No defence
Read Matthew 27:11-14

❓ *Why does Jesus not reply to the charges?*
❓ *Why is Pilate surprised by this?*

Barabbas
Read Matthew 27:15-21

❓ *What is Pilate's dilemma?*
❓ *How does Pilate try to wriggle out of his dilemma?*
❓ *Why do you think the crowds are so hostile? What motivates them?*

It's an appalling scene. Don't you feel angry that such a cry could ever be heard? It's true that the weak crowd were influenced by the evil and powerful chief priests; it's true that they, as well as Pilate, were taking the coward's way out—but what a terrible choice. The coward's escape route had gone horribly wrong. Now Pilate did not just have some bitter Jews to deal with, but the knowledge that he would be guilty of the blood of an innocent man—and one whose disturbing claim was to be the Son of God. Remember Pilate when you are tempted to take a spineless decision to avoid opposition.

Crucify

Read Matthew 27:22-23

Sense the evil as they chant their murderous demands. Crowds of people, many of whom had probably never harmed anyone in their lives, suddenly turn into murderers when it comes to the Son of God, the Saviour of the world.

❓ *Why is that?*

There was one man who was terrified by the yelling mob. Not Jesus, who stands calm and determined, but Pilate. Pathetically he tries to shift the blame to ease his searing conscience...

Guilt sticks
Read Matthew 27:24-26

❓ *Why does Pilate wash his hands?*
❓ *Why is the crowd's reply important?*

Guilt cannot just be given away. Pilate surely knew that. He knew that he, as well as Jesus, was now condemned. But it is clear that it is the people who have driven Jesus to death, even though it is by the hand of the Roman governor. Israel rejects its one true King.

⌃ Pray

Ask the Lord to give you the boldness to do the right thing, even when the crowd is against you.

Praise God for his perfect plan, unfolding precisely as predicted in the Scriptures.

Crown him

Bruised and lacerated from the cruel Roman scourging, the King now becomes the object of ridicule for a crowd of brutal soldiers.

Crowning the King

Read Matthew 27:27-30

- ❓ *What is the significance of the items they dress Jesus up in?*
- ❓ *What is the powerful and terrible irony in this scene—how do you see it?*

To an unknowing observer this must have been a pathetic and ludicrous scene. The tattered "royal" robe, the crude thorny crown, the weak reed for a sceptre, the mocking chorus. But for those of us who understand, we see something quite different. Not that we are indifferent to the humiliation of our Lord. But we see our King arrayed in his glory, we see the beauty and majesty of the one who is abused and derided. For who but the King of kings would bear this vile treatment as he did? Awesome majesty!

⌃ Pray

Take a moment to praise our Lord for the way he endured this humiliation for us all.

Crucifying the King

Matthew 27:31-37

- ❓ *What strikes you about the way the crucifixion is described?*
- ❓ *What details do you find intriguing?*

The story is told in a very matter-of-fact way. The Gospel writers don't want to tell a story of cruelty and injustice to make us feel sorry for Jesus. The Roman cross is, of course, horrific. But there is something much bigger going on that we need to focus our gaze on. A suffering beyond the details of blood and wood and nails. The pain of crucifixion was so intense that a strong drink was generally given to numb the body a little (v 34).

- ❓ *Why do you think Jesus refused this?*
- ❓ *Drink in the details. What are your conflicting emotions as you ponder it?*

Jesus' crime was to claim to be the promised King of the Jews. To the hardened, foolish crowd, the mocking sign didn't seem out of place (v 37). And there was no indignity spared to the lowest of criminals—see v 35-36. Exposed, he hung there, while at his feet some gambled over his clothes, and others sat staring, gloating—in debased delight.

The real pain

Read Galatians 3:13

God's own curse, upon his own dear Son. The torture and shame of the cross were easy to bear compared to this. While others gawked, his Father's wrath was poured out on him. It was the curse that we deserved, the anger that was due for his people's sins and not his own.

⌃ Pray

Is this your King? Then crown him—not with thorns, but in your heart.

Bitter hatred

It is possible to know all the facts about Jesus and yet despise him, jeer at him and hate him.

Give us proof!

Read Matthew 27:38-44

- ❓ *Why do you think this mockery is reported in such detail here?*
- ❓ *What do they think Jesus' helplessness proves?*
- ❓ *If he had come down from the cross, would they have believed him (v 42)?*
- ❓ *If he had come down, what would it actually prove (see 26:53-54)?*

Many today demand proof that Jesus is the Son of God—certainly they would believe then! And yet that was the very reason many of the Jews were so violently opposed to Jesus. His miracles, his healings, his authority, his holiness—done in plain sight for three years of ministry—all pointed clearly to the inescapable truth: this was indeed the Son of God. Would further evidence really convince them as they claimed? No, that would have shown up their own evil even more clearly, and intensified still further their hatred of him.

- ❓ *How can we be sure of that? Look ahead to 28:6, 11-15.*

Here was the ultimate evidence; not merely coming off the cross, but out of the grave itself! But no amount of proof changes hard, unbelieving hearts.

All alike

Re-read Matthew 27:38-44

Think again about this awful scene.

- ❓ *Do you think these people were exceptional? Would another crowd really have reacted very differently?*
- ❓ *How can we see this as a picture of the way people still treat Christ today?*

These verses are a vivid picture of the way the Saviour is treated today. Not literally perhaps, not even openly, but in the hearts of all who know that Jesus shows up their sin, that Jesus condemns them, that he truly is the Son of God.

For those who demand proof, point them to the unanswerable proof of Jesus' death and resurrection. The facts are there, but will they examine them? Will they take the time to think about them? Will they believe them? And will they put their trust in the one who so clearly is the Son of God?

☑ Apply

- ❓ *Do you care about the way others speak and think of the Saviour?*
- ❓ *How can we best show it?*
- ❓ *What is your reaction when people use the precious name "Jesus" as a swear word?*
- ❓ *When should we/shouldn't we make a response to that?*

Ultimate agony

Picture the appalling scene again: Jesus hanging in agony; crowds jeering loudly; midday sun blazing down—and then...

The sun hides its face

Read Matthew 27:45

❓ *What does the darkness signify?*

Blackness, coldness, fear. The darkness of God's judgment and wrath. No doubt the mocking faded out into astonished silence. But the wrath was not directed at the crowds...

Think of the sufferings Jesus had already endured. The betrayal, the denial, the desertion. The injustice, the scourging, the spitting, the derision, the shame. The cross itself—with all its excruciating pain. But all along something had been uppermost in Jesus' mind. All these gruelling experiences were overshadowed by one horrific prospect. All the time he knew he must drink the bitter cup; but now that "hell" had come, the darkness of the Father's anger was on him.

Father hides his face

Read Matthew 27:46

❓ *How does Jesus' cry reveal the hidden agony of the cross?*

Aloneness. Desolation. For those agonising hours he did not enjoy his Father's presence and support—he bore alone that colossal load of sin. "Why have you forsaken me?" It was for his people he had to suffer; to bear the whole punishment for their foul sins. Nothing less than the experience of eternal

hell could be sufficient; the hell of being God-forsaken, of having the eternal anger of his Father poured out on their sin, the sin Jesus was bearing in himself.

We simply cannot understand. We cannot expect to. Infinite agony crowded into three hours. No wonder the sun went black. Creation itself was groaning, while the bystanders could only jeer.

Read Matthew 27:47-49

···**TIME OUT**·································

If you have time, **read Psalm 22:1-11** slowly, and see how this is the key to understanding the meaning of the cross.

⌃ Pray

We cannot understand; but we can be amazed. And we can consider whether it was for our sins. And when we know it was, we can contemplate his infinite love for us...

I sometimes think about the cross,
and shut my eyes and try to see the cruel nails,
and crown of thorns,
and Jesus crucified for me.

But, even could I see Him die,
I could but see a little part
of that great love which, like a fire,
is always burning in His heart.

W.W. How

It is finished

The darkness was over. The crowds could once again shake off the fears and the questions that must have been provoked by the strange events of the last three hours.

Perhaps now they could enjoy the rest of the crucifixion in peace. But for Jesus the great work had been done...

All over

Read Matthew 27:50

❷ *What is unusual about Jesus' death?*

It is true that he must still face death and the grave—those vivid consequences of the sin that was so abhorrent to him. Yet the experience he had so shrunk from was over. His Father's anger had been borne; once more he could know his smile upon him, never to be lost again. The Lord Jesus was ready to give up his spirit into his Father's care. The crowds prepare to go home, no doubt puzzled, but still with hard and unbelieving hearts. But before they leave, something else happens to unsettle their mocking confidence.

Heartquake

Read Matthew 27:51-54

❷ *What is the meaning of each of the powerful signs that accompany Jesus' death?*
❷ *What is ironic about verse 54?*

It's as if God's world is shaking with awe (or is it celebration?) at what has happened. Rocks split apart, graves open up, dead bones awake. Death works backwards. And the great curtain separating worshippers

from the holy presence of God is triumphantly ripped open by heaven's hand. God is speaking, in dramatic style, in language that no one could mistake.

This is a moment of victory, not defeat; of glory, not shame; of purpose, not waste. The sin-barrier has been torn down, heaven's door has been thrown open. God is vindicating his dearly loved Son. And some listened. Some feared. Some saw at last who they had crucified. Not the "people of God", the hyper-religious Jews. Instead, it is hard-bitten, irreligious Roman soldiers who declare Jesus to be God's Son

⌄ Apply

❷ *What is the warning and the promise for us in these verses?*

Many start well, but slip back into religious (not righteous!) living and thinking. You read your Bible, but are you still shaken by these events? Your heart, though religious, may be even more resistant than those of the foul-mouthed atheists around you.

And is your heart growing harder still as you read more, hear more, understand more, and perhaps resist more?

⌃ Pray

Talk to the Lord about your thoughts now.

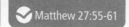
Who cared?

Not all had relished Jesus' agony and death. Some cared deeply for him...

The women
Read Matthew 27:55-56

❓ *Who cared enough to stay close?*
❓ *Who is missing from this list?*

There is no mention of the eleven disciples, although John at least was there (see John 19:25-27). Many of these women are not famous—their names are not recorded. No doubt they longed to be able to do something for him. But now they were helpless; they could do no more than be there with him, watching sadly.

Joseph
Read Matthew 27:57-60

❓ *Who is missing again?*
❓ *Why is Jesus' burial so important?*
❓ *What do you think motivated Joseph to do what he did?*

No mention of bold Peter. Joseph was a secret disciple, who feared the Jews (see John 19:38). Yet now love compelled him; overcoming his weakness and fear. And so he devotes his unopened, unspoiled tomb for his Lord.

⌄ Apply

Not many could have done that for Jesus—most of his disciples were poor. Jesus has a use for each one of his people.

❓ *Is there something that only you can do for him; and yet it seems so costly?*

If you care about his death, then follow the "fearful" Joseph and be bold in your service to the Lord you love.

Mary and Mary
Read Matthew 27:61

❓ *Who is missing again here?*

No mention of those who had been the closest followers of Jesus—the disciples; just two people who loved Jesus. They mourned by the tomb. They could not leave his dead body. They did not yet understand that he had to die so that their sins could be forgiven. They did not believe that soon he would rise from that grave. And yet both women must have had a strong sense that this was possible.

⌄ Apply

We need not mourn over Jesus' body, for he is risen! But it is right to mourn over the sins that brought him to the grave. If we do care about his death, we will not only sorrow over our sins but leave them in the grave. **Read Romans 6:8-13.**

It was not the ones who we would have expected that cared most for their Lord. It is those who are "least" who are counted greatest in the kingdom of God.

Resurrection day

The Jews were worried. They had seen some amazing events which must have shaken their confidence. But what if Jesus did rise from the dead as he had said?

Worried
Read Matthew 27:62-66

❷ *What are the authorities worried about?*

❷ *What plan do they hatch to ensure that Jesus "stays dead"?*

It would be the worst possible scenario for them—all their public credibility would be lost, they would be humiliated. Such an occurrence must be prevented at all costs. They were also worried that the disciples might fake a resurrection. But that would hardly convince the people, unless they could produce a living, breathing Messiah. Perhaps it was the prospect of a real resurrection that troubled the Jews most.

Unbelieving
Read Matthew 28:1

❷ *How might these women have been feeling as they came to the tomb?*

❷ *What might they have been thinking?*

In their time of mourning, two women—faithful followers of Jesus—decided to rise early to gaze on the tomb of their Lord. We know from other Gospel accounts that their only concern was how they would roll away the stone. It never crossed their minds that they might not need to.

Their faith in the repeated predictions of their Lord was zero at this point. They had simply blanked out from their minds his repeated teaching that he would die and rise on the third day. They had forgotten the raising of Lazarus and others, and his words claiming to be the resurrection and the life. God was seeing to it that there could be no reasonable doubt about the resurrection of his Son; that any suspicion of the disciples stealing Jesus' body would be totally unfounded. The very thing the Jews were so anxious to avoid, they were unknowingly guaranteeing—the possibility of the disciples "fixing" it was eliminated.

Risen
Read Matthew 28:2-4

❷ *What happens and what does it signify?*

The drama of another earthquake and a shining angel is nothing compared with what goes undescribed. What left the guards shaking, and what will shake the world again, is that Jesus is risen! Ever since the day that sin came into the world, death had reigned supreme. Now death had been conquered! Jesus had risen to die no more! This Sunday morning was the pivotal day in world history. His enemies feared it, his disciples wouldn't believe it—and yet it happened. Hope and joy and eternal life spring from the risen Saviour—God's answer to sin and death and damnation. And yet the world still doesn't know it!

❷ *What are you doing to convince others about what happened that day?*

No room for doubt

Anyone watching the two Marys start out to the tomb, and then noticing them again on their return, would have been astonished.

Read Matthew 28:5-10

- ❷ *Follow through the emotions of the two women from grief to fear to a strange mixture of fear, joy and worship.*
- ❷ *Can you understand how they felt?*
- ❷ *How does the Lord help his followers deal with their bewildering experience?*

They had arrived in Jerusalem a week earlier filled with hope, which had been cruelly dashed. It is hard to trust again when you have been so brutally disappointed. But now it all seemed too good to be true; surely any moment all their hopes would be dashed. Notice how Jesus helps his followers...

Dispelling doubts

- ❷ *What six pieces of tangible evidence does Jesus give them?*

Shouldn't it have been enough just to have been told by an angel?! Jesus knew just how much proof they needed; things they could look back on and know that the truth of his rising was undeniable.

- ❷ *How is that an encouragement when our faith is so weak, and we are slow to take God's word for it?*

Words of love

- ❷ *What is Jesus' tone with his followers?*
- ❷ *How else could he have spoken to them?*

The Lord Jesus is so kind. The women—like the rest of the disciples—had not believed Jesus. They held out no hope of him rising from the dead, as he had said. So does Jesus reprove them? Does he do anything but encourage them?

- ❷ *Can you praise God for times when your faith has been at its lowest but God's love has shone brightest?*

Restoration

- ❷ *What does Jesus show to them about their continuing relationship with him?*

He will restore his disciples. They had deserted him—being cowardly as well as unbelieving. They had not even shown love for him at the cross and at his tomb. *But Jesus had not deserted them.* He would prove to them too that he had risen (v 10); for he knew they would not have enough faith to believe the two Marys.

Suppressing the truth

Read Matthew 28:11-15

- ❷ *What contrast is being drawn here?*

How differently Jesus will treat those who struggle to believe, and those who deny what they know to be true. And yet God's grace even reaches some of them.

Spread the news

Jesus has risen! Salvation for all nations! But who was going to spread the good news? Jesus must soon return to his Father; who was left?

Eleven weak, frightened, disbelieving, discouraged disciples. Devastated by the death of their Lord, in hiding for fear of the Jews and reluctant to believe the reports of Jesus' resurrection. These ordinary people were soon going to challenge a hostile world with their message. What changed them?

Read Matthew 28:16-20

> ❷ *What aspects of Jesus' words in verses 18-20 would have really helped them?*
> ❷ *Which of these do you find personally most compelling?*

- **Jesus' presence (v 17).** To see Jesus was enough for most of them. Now they could believe the amazing fact. These men were now qualified as eye-witnesses of his resurrection.

- **Jesus' power (v 18).** They had been given his power before when they went out two by two. Now they had fresh vivid evidence that he is Almighty God. The one giving the command has been given all authority and power—how could they do anything but obey? And what an encouragement that their mission was backed by him!

- **Jesus' purpose (v 19).** No longer a mission only to the Jews. The whole world is to know. Jesus' purpose must be their purpose; to make disciples out of all nations, teaching all that he had taught them.

- **Jesus' promise (v 20).** "I am with you always". That must have seemed strange to the disciples, for Jesus was about to leave

them. But they believed his promise this time, so when Jesus ascended they were not crushed and disappointed.

····**TIME OUT**····································

Read Luke 24:45-53. Matthew is not explicit about it, but what a change these last few verses in Luke show! Jesus' words transformed these men. But the transformation was not complete; not until they had actually received that promise of Jesus, his Holy Spirit coming in power upon them.

> ❷ *Is that the kind of transformation you look for—individually, in your church, in our country?*

⌃ Pray

Pray for more of his Holy Spirit, more of his power strengthening you to obey his will, and more of his purpose in your heart to reach people everywhere with the gospel.

And if you are feeling feeble, useless and scared—much like the eleven—then know that you can be God's instrument to spread the joyful news to the world that Jesus is alive and reigns for ever.

PHILEMON: Five journeys

This short, personal letter from Paul to his friend Philemon gives us a snapshot picture of how the gospel shapes our lives, characters and decisions. Over the next few days we'll follow five different journeys in the story…

Read the whole of Philemon

Journey 1: the letter

❷ *What is the general tone of this letter?*
❷ *Can you pick up the details of the basic story behind it?*

Long story short: rebel slave Onesimus has stolen from, and run away from his master, Philemon. Incredibly, he ends up meeting Paul, probably in Rome, where he becomes a Christian. Paul sends him back to his old friend Philemon with this letter—asking him to accept Onesimus as a Christian brother, and not have him put to death as a runaway slave.

Paul: the sender

Re-read Philemon 1-3

❷ *What is Paul's situation as he writes?*
❷ *Given the "Onesimus problem", how do you think Paul would be feeling as he writes?*

Apphia is probably Philemon's wife. Archippus may have lived with them—it seems that the Colossian church met in their house (v 2). But perhaps Paul mentions Archippus to make Philemon aware that the big decision he is about to take over the runaway slave is not something he can do in isolation. It is a decision that he makes as part of the body of Christ, and it will affect his brothers and sisters in the church.

⌄ Apply

Most of us tend to make major life decisions by ourselves.

❷ *How could we include our church family and leadership in the way we make our choices?*

Journey 2: Philemon

Re-read Philemon 4-7

❷ *What kind of Christian is Philemon?*
❷ *How does Paul feel when he thinks about him?*

Some Christians, even keen ones, can be a bit of a burden to be with. But to be in Philemon's presence was to be refreshed.

Philemon is clearly a brilliant guy; great to be around; an asset to any church. But even he needs to grow—he hasn't reached journey's end in his Christian life.

❷ *What next step is Paul praying for Philemon?*
❷ *What's the promise in verse 6?*

⌃ Pray

Pray the same thing for yourself today…

From rebel to redeemed

Slavery in the ancient world was very different to the slavery of the 18th century or today. More than half the Roman population were slaves, and many rose to positions of great responsibility.

Journey 3: Onesimus

Read Philemon 8-12, 18

❓ *What was Onesimus like as a slave (see v 11, 18)?*

❓ *How does Paul describe his relationship with Onesimus?*

❓ *How has the gospel changed Onesimus?*

Chalk and cheese, as we say in Britain. Apples and oranges, as Americans might put it. In God's amazing providence, this rebellious thief of a runaway slave somehow finds himself with the imprisoned apostle. He hears from him how Jesus can set him free from a far worse slavery than is his by social status. He becomes Paul's spiritual "son" as he becomes a believer. He discovers a family, acceptance, friendship and forgiveness that he has never known before. *Wonderful!*

The name Onesimus means "useful"; a slave name that up to this point had been rather ironic. But finding Christ means that he has become willing to serve and work, because his new master—the Lord Jesus—was willing to serve him, and work for his salvation on the cross, and buy him back from slavery to sin at the astonishing cost of his own blood (see Ephesians 1:7).

Jesus has made him truly himself—he has brought together his name and his character. He is no longer use*less*, but use*ful* to such an extent that Paul wants to hang on to him (Philemon 13).

✔ Apply

God is in the business of changing people by his Spirit. He takes useless people, who were only ever serving themselves, and turns them into the image of his Son: people who love to serve and love others.

❓ *Are you still making progress in that journey as a Christian? Or have you slipped back into old ways of pleasing yourself, laziness, or cutting corners?*

⌃ Pray

Thank God that the gospel of grace is such good news for rebels like us. Pray that you would:

- know more clearly today all you have been given in Christ
- be changed deep down by that understanding, and
- have an opportunity to share your faith today with someone.

Lord, I want to be useful to you. Please lead me to someone I can serve today, for Jesus' sake. Amen.

From tyrant to servant

An apostle is someone who has been personally sent by Jesus, and carries all the authority of Christ in his words and commands. It's surprising, then, to see how Paul argues his case here.

Journey 4: Paul

Read Philemon 8-21

❓ *What does Paul appeal to in order to convince Philemon to accept Onesimus back into his household (v 9)?*

❓ *What does he specifically choose not to do (v 8)?*

❓ *Why do you think that is?*

It's worth thinking about how the apostle argues here, and how the gospel of grace has done its work on his heart. As Saul, this man was a determined tyrant who commanded troops of soldiers to ruthlessly oppress the Christians he so hated. Now, like his new master, he is happy to lay aside his rights, and win others by his example of love and service. Notice that:

- **Paul prefers the arguments of love to apostolic authority.** He could have demanded, but he preferred to plead. He wanted to treat Philemon as a dear brother, rather than ruling over him.

- **Paul's arguments are passionate and persuasive.** A loving approach does not need to be a spineless, flabby one. Despite the fact that he stands to lose personally, Paul's appeal is crammed full of potent reason.

- **Paul's arguments are full of tact and humour.** Not of flattery and dishonesty, but designed with Philemon's feelings in mind—yet without losing any of their force.

⌄ Apply

❓ *What tricky situations are you trying to navigate at the moment with family, community or church?*

❓ *What is your natural instinct as a way to argue your viewpoint?*

❓ *What might you learn from Paul's approach here about how to conduct yourself in these kinds of discussions?*

⌃ Pray

Pray for anyone in leadership in your church. Ask God to help them serve with tact and humility.

And pray for yourself as you relate to other believers. Ask God to help you encourage others, and not browbeat them into submission.

From blessing to betrayal

In some ways, Philemon is an agonising letter to read because—this side of eternity—we can't know how this story ended...

A final appeal
Read Philemon 17-21

❓ *What final things does Paul say to persuade Philemon to receive Onesimus as a brother?*

❓ *What conflicting emotions do you think Philemon might have as he reads this letter?*

Onesimus's offence is great. Philemon had every legal right—and plenty of reason—to have him put to death, or at least severely punished. This is no easy choice for Philemon. Applying the gospel to this decision would put him at radical odds with the culture, and perhaps his pagan friends and business associates. His neighbours would say: "What a terrible example to other slaves!" "Wrongdoing deserves punishment!" Perhaps he read the letter with a furrowed brow.

So there is gospel-soaked reason even in these final appeals by Paul. He reminds Philemon of his own debt of his life to Paul, and of their bond as brothers in Christ. And, following Christ's example, Paul even offers himself as a substitute, for the financial consequences of the sins of Onesimus: "I will pay it back" (v 19).

He includes a warm-hearted joke. The word "refresh" in v 20 is from the same root as the name Onesimus. He is literally saying: "Onesimise my heart in Christ!"

Journey 5: Demas
Read Philemon 22-25

❓ *What is impressive about the people mentioned in verses 23-24 (see Colossians 4:10, 12-14)?*

This is almost certainly the band who were with Paul while he was under house arrest in Rome (Acts 28:30-31). It was a house filled with gospel writers (Luke, Mark and Paul), where the gospel of Christ was proclaimed unhindered, and people laboured in prayer for the church as it faced conflict and opposition. What an exciting place to be! What a privilege to be part of such a dynamic, creative, hard-working gospel community!

Read 2 Timothy 4:10

❓ *What happened to Demas? Why?*

❓ *What's the warning for us?*

Demas was at the heart of this community, where the Holy Spirit was inspiring the very words of Scripture. But he was not immune to unbelief and worldly temptation. Demas's sad journey is a warning to us all. You may be at the heart of a vibrant church, running successful groups, seeing the Lord do amazing things. But we need to guard our hearts and, as we have seen in this little letter, allow the gospel to continue to shape our thoughts and decisions.

> *If you think you are standing firm, be careful that you don't fall.*
> 1 Corinthians 10:12

David's school of prayer

In this "disaster sandwich" psalm, the bread is the cries for help and rescue from his enemies. The tasty filling shows us what a godly person truly desires.

Together they teach us some important lessons on how to pray

Read Psalm 25

Pray where you are

❓ *What and how does David pray?*

No pious, high-sounding formulae, like you sometimes hear at prayer meetings. David starts with a heartfelt cry about the things that dominate his horizons (v 2, 3).

⌃ Pray

❓ *What is going on with you right now?*

Explain your situation to God. It might seem a bit silly— because he knows it all already. But there's a good reason for it. Simply recounting the difficulty or dilemma, and laying it before God starts to change how we see it.

Pray when you don't feel like it

Don't wait for a good mood to start praying (v 16, 17): actually you need to pray most when you least feel like it! We avoid God's face when we've made up our minds to sin. David knows he needs God's help to stay pure (v 4-5). The temptation to retaliate against opposition is so strong that he needs supernatural help to resist it.

⌄ Apply

Be disciplined in prayer. It's the only way to keep at it when you don't want to. Having a regular time, a prayer partner, or being committed to a prayer meeting are all ways to make sure that you come before the Lord when you most need it, and least want to.

Spend a moment talking honestly with God about the things you are feeling—even if that is coldness, indifference and a lack of motivation.

Pray for others too

❓ *How do verses 8-10 help us keep motivated?*

Our prayers can become self-centred and self-focused, but keeping the right view of God (v 8-10) must lead us into God's wider purposes (v 22).

Praise the Lord using the words of verses 8-10. You will be reminding yourself who you are speaking to, and how he will hear and respond to your requests.

Now pray for others in need, and especially for those who are serving God's purposes in your country and around the world.

ISAIAH:
The coming of God

Isaiah wrote in the 8th century BC. But in chapters 40 – 55 he looks forward 200 years to the coming exile in Babylon.

As refugees, taken away from their homeland, Isaiah's readers faced a crisis of faith. *Perhaps God is powerless. Or perhaps he has abandoned us. He's indifferent to our plight.*

❓ *What makes people say this kind of thing today? Who do you know who may be thinking this way?*

But Isaiah has a message of comfort (40:1). What is this comfort? The answer comes in verse 9: "Here is your God!"

Read Isaiah 40:1-11

❓ *What is God like in verses 10-11?*
❓ *How do you think those who were in exile would have felt to hear this message?*

Prepare the way

❓ *What does the voice Isaiah hears call for (v 3)?*
❓ *What will happen (v 4)?*
❓ *What's all this for (v 5)?*

It seems Isaiah has in mind a processional route. It's a royal event where the roads are swept, banners are hung and everything is prepared so the royal carriage can parade through the streets. Here the route is being prepared for the coming of the King: God himself, coming to rule his people.

God's reward

In verses 1-2, Isaiah says that Israel's sin has been paid for. ("Double" here doesn't mean that God has demanded twice what is owed. It's more that the debt has its double—it has been matched by the payment.) The punishment is finished. Is that right? In one sense, yes. The punishment that God had decreed—70 years of exile—would reach its end. And yet the underlying problem of sin still remained.

So why could Isaiah speak comfort to the exiles? Because he was promising that God would come to pay the price of sin once and for all.

Here is the King

Mark 1:3-4 quotes Isaiah 40:3 and then says, "And so John the Baptist appeared in the wilderness". In other words, the "voice" is the voice of John the Baptist. And that means the Sovereign Lord coming to his people is Jesus. The God who comes with power to rule is Jesus.

☑ Apply

❓ *How could you use this passage to sum up why Jesus came?*
❓ *What words of comfort about Jesus could you bring to those around you today?*

The shepherd's voice

We're not quite done yet with Isaiah's vision of the coming King.

This is our good news: God comes in Christ, and God deals with sin in Christ. But God also gathers his people in Christ.

Re-read Isaiah 40:1-11

> ❷ *What four things does God do in verse 11?*

Jesus described himself as the Good Shepherd. That's the picture we see here.

How does Jesus gather and tend his sheep? He said that the Good Shepherd "calls his own sheep by name ... and his sheep follow him because they know his voice" (John 10:3-4). He gathers his sheep by his word.

The word of our God

Isaiah 40:6-8 tells us something about the nature of that word.

> ❷ *What is God's word like?*
> ❷ *Why is that better than human words?*
> ❷ *Why would this message have encouraged those who were in exile?*
> ❷ *What do you find encouraging about it personally today?*

The word preached

Verses 6-8 might sound familiar. That's because they're quoted in 1 Peter.

Read 1 Peter 1:23-25

> ❷ *What has happened because of the word of God (v 23)?*

> ❷ *What is this word (v 25)?*

You and I have a role to play in Jesus' gathering of his people. God's word is now preached by human voices. We speak, and people hear the voice of Jesus. No wonder Isaiah says, "Lift up your voice". When you lift up your voice, for some people it will be the voice of the Good Shepherd. What goes in their ears might be the sound of your voice, talking about Jesus over a cup of tea. But what they hear will be the voice of the Good Shepherd.

All this explains why Jesus sends us out in mission—whether to the friends and neighbours we already live among, or to the ends of the earth. It's so that he can gather his sheep.

⌃ Pray

Spend time praising God for his enduring word and the difference it has made in your life. Ask God to help you to use your words to speak of Jesus to others. Ask him to give you opportunities to do so, even today. Pray for your brothers and sisters in Christ—whether near or far away—and ask God to give them words to say that speak about Jesus, too.

Beyond compare

"Here is your God", Isaiah has said—and he still has more to tell us about what this God is like.

The big theme of Isaiah 40 – 55 is that the Lord will redeem his people and lead them home to demonstrate that he is beyond compare. He alone is enthroned above the earth, and the nations are as nothing before him.

Read Isaiah 40:12-26

> ❷ *What are the answers to the questions in verses 12-14?*
> ❷ *What comparison is Isaiah making in verses 15-17?*
> ❷ *What comparison is he mocking in verses 18-20?*
> ❷ *How do verses 21-26 prove that worshipping idols is ridiculous?*

Where is God?

Read Isaiah 40:27-31

Verse 27 reveals why Isaiah's audience needed to hear this lesson about God's supremacy.

> ❷ *What are they saying (v 27)?*
> ❷ *What's Isaiah's response (v 28)?*
> ❷ *What's his promise (v 29-31)?*

▽ Apply

> ❷ *In what situations do you need greater confidence in God?*
> ❷ *How does this message comfort and help you?*
> ❷ *What will you change about the way you think or act?*

God of history

Having promised strength to his people in 40:29-31, God then calls on the nations to renew their strength so they are ready to participate in a court case with him (41:1).

Read Isaiah 41:1-14

> ❷ *Where do the nations seek to draw strength from (v 5-7)?*
> ❷ *But where do God's people draw their strength from (v 9-10)?*
> ❷ *So what does he promise will happen (v 11-14)?*

In chapters 1 – 39 the fact that the Lord is "the Holy One of Israel" was a reason for his discipline against unholy Israel. But now this name becomes the reason for his redemption of his people, for the holy God will be true to his covenant commitments.

⌃ Pray

> ❷ *How do you respond to the thought of being like a "worm" (41:14) by comparison with God?*

Spend some time in prayer to God about this, expressing your dependence on him and need for his help.

The next six studies will pick up speed and take a highlights tour through the rest of Isaiah 40 – 48. You may like to read the sections we miss out. See if you can spot the same themes recurring throughout.

Here is my servant

We're about to be introduced to one of the key characters of the book of Isaiah. But it might surprise you who it turns out to be…

This is the other key focus of Isaiah 40 – 55: the Servant of the Lord, who is introduced in four "songs", the first of which is found in 42:1-9.

Read Isaiah 42:1-9

- ❷ *What is the relationship between God ("I") and the Servant (v 1, 6)?*
- ❷ *In verses 2-4, what will the Servant not do?*
- ❷ *What will he come to do (v 4, 6, 7)?*
- ❷ *What words would you use to describe the Servant in these verses?*

Greeting the champion

Read Isaiah 42:10-17

- ❷ *How should people respond to the coming of the Lord (v 10-12)?*

God marches forth like a warrior to rescue (v 13).

- ❷ *Who is he rescuing (v 16)?*
- ❷ *What will happen to those who do not trust in God (v 17)?*

But who?

In these songs, it sometimes seems that the Servant is Israel. The nation of Israel was called to serve God by revealing him to the nations. But sometimes the Servant appears to be an individual who redeems Israel.

Read Isaiah 42:18-25

In verse 19 it's clear that the Lord's Servant is Israel. God's people aren't a good servant— they are the blind person from verse 16!

- ❷ *What has happened to Israel as a result (v 22, 25)?*

The nation of Israel cannot properly fulfil the role of God's Servant. Into this void, as we'll see in the following chapters, steps Cyrus, a foreign king who is nevertheless described as God's shepherd and anointed (literally his "messiah", 45:1). The task of Cyrus as God's servant is the liberation of Judah from exile.

But Isaiah also promises an ultimate Servant, who will accomplish the ultimate liberation of all God's people through his own suffering and death (52:13 – 53:12). He is of course talking about Jesus.

Jesus also renews the witness of his people. In Acts 13:47, Paul applies Isaiah 49:6 to his own mission. Israel was supposed to be God's witness but failed. But now, through Christ, the church is the servant of God, witnessing to him among the nations.

☑ Apply

- ❷ *We can't do everything Jesus did. But how does Isaiah 42:1-7 illustrate what it might look like for us to be like Jesus?*
- ❷ *How might we fall into the traps Israel fell into? How can we avoid this?*

Called and created

It can be hard sometimes to shake off the feeling of not belonging. We often worry about whether we make the grade. In all sorts of situations, we don't feel at home.

As we've seen, Isaiah is looking ahead to the time of the Babylonian exile. God's people would not make the grade. They would go away into exile. They would not feel at home because they would not be at home. But Isaiah is looking beyond this moment of judgment to offer hope.

Read Isaiah 43:1-7

"I have redeemed you," says 43:1. It's the language that was used of the exodus. God redeemed Israel from slavery in Egypt just as someone would have redeemed (or "bought back") a slave from the slave market.

❷ *What "waters" did Israel pass through to get out of Egypt and into the promised land (see Exodus 14; Joshua 3 – 4)?*

Isaiah is looking back to the exodus as a precedent or, better still, a blueprint for what God will do in the future.

The flames in Isaiah 43:2 don't come from the exodus story, however.

Re-read Isaiah 42:24-25

❷ *What do the flames represent here? Who causes them?*

People are surrounded by judgment. But the new exodus will deliver us from God's judgment.

On a different scale

❷ *Where will God's people be gathered from (43:5-7)?*

This description goes well beyond the return from Babylonian exile. It's pointing forward to something greater.

Throughout the New Testament the work of Jesus is described using exodus or new-exodus language—particularly language about "redemption" (Romans 3:24; Colossians 1:13-14) and "inheritance" (1 Peter 1:3-5). Jesus has redeemed us or bought us to be his own people. He is giving us an inheritance in the new creation, just as he gave Israel an inheritance in the promised land.

His very own

❷ *What is the similarity between Isaiah 43:1 and 7?*

This is not a reference to the creation of the world but to the creation of Israel as God's people, through the exodus. We can also apply it to ourselves, who have been redeemed and newly created in Christ.

⌃ Pray

It's striking how intimate the language in verses 1-4 is. Spend some time pausing over it. Maybe you feel like you're sinking or being overwhelmed by life. Maybe you're feeling the heat. Hear God speaking these words to you today. Then pray for others that they would know these same truths.

Put to the test

The language of "gathering" continues in the next section of Isaiah 43. But this gathering is very different.

God is summoning the nations to a court case. At first it looks like it's God himself who is on trial—but then he brings his accusation against the false gods of the nations.

Read Isaiah 43:8-13

- ❓ *Who comes to the trial (v 9)?*
- ❓ *How are they described (v 8)?*
- ❓ *What are they bringing witnesses to prove (v 9)?*
- ❓ *What does God bring witnesses to prove (v 10-13)?*
- ❓ *What evidence does he call upon (v 12-13)?*

Future proof

God's ability to speak of the future is presented again and again in these chapters.

Read Isaiah 41:21-27

- ❓ *What does God invite the false gods to do (v 22-23)?*
- ❓ *Can they do it?*
- ❓ *What is God doing (v 25)?*
- ❓ *What does this prove about God, and why (v 26-27)?*

When we compare the one true God with any other gods or ideologies, what do we see? God is the Creator (43:10), the Saviour (v 11), and the revealer of the future (v 12). What he does, no one can undo (v 13).

⌃ Pray

Spend time praising God for who he has proved himself to be. Commit yourself to him afresh—the only true God.

Call the witness

In Isaiah 43, the witnesses for God's defence are God's people (v 12). The problem is that humanity is the judge, and humanity is blind and deaf (v 8).

It matters what you and I tell people about our experience of God. We testify to him before humanity. But God is the only one who can reveal the truth (v 12)—the only one who can open blind eyes and deaf ears so that people receive our message about him.

⌄ Apply

"You are my witnesses ... that I am God" (v 12).

- ❓ *What can you testify about what God has done?*
- ❓ *What are you confident he will do?*
- ❓ *What does this prove about who he is and what he is like?*
- ❓ *Who could you tell about these things this week?*

Grasping in the dark

You may have heard it said that the person who is closest to God is the one who is most aware of their own sinfulness. That thought seems a long way away from David.

Read Psalm 26

> ❓ *What does David say about his own commitment to God?*
> ❓ *What is the big claim he makes (v 11)?*

It seems as if he's boasting to God about: how much he trusts him (v 1); his (not God's) faithfulness (v 2-3); his hatred of wrong and wrongdoers (v 4-6); and his love of God, and God's house (v 7-8). In a word, he describes himself as "blameless" (v 11). This is the kind of language that would cause people to stare at you in horror if you came out with it at a prayer meeting.

> ❓ *How do you react to this confident attitude?*

What's the question?

The key to understanding the psalm is working out the question he is wrestling with. He has strived to live a life that honours God. He has avoided evil. He has attended diligently to his spiritual life.

> ❓ *So what's his problem (v 9, 10)?*

David is worried that, despite all his efforts to be righteous, God will judge him along with all the evildoers, and sweep them both away. Verses 4-5 echo the marks of the "blessed man" in Psalm 1:1. David has believed the first half of the psalm, but doesn't seem to believe God's promise at the end (see Psalm 1:6).

His problem is that, despite his apparent righteousness, he sees that God's judgment will cut through every pretence of righteousness for the filthy rags that they are. Is it worth following God if I am swept away with the rest of the rubbish when judgment comes?

✔ Apply

These kinds of doubts can torture ordinary believers too. *Can I really be forgiven?* Despite my outward show of godliness, I know the blackness of my heart, so the Lord my Judge must see it too.

> ❓ *What might you say to a believer who struggles with these thoughts?*

What's the answer?

David is grasping in the dark for the answer to his question— he cannot see Christ clearly. But along the way he grabs hold of some good things:

> ❓ *What are they (Psalm 26:11-12)?*

▲ Pray

Praise God that, in Christ, your feet stand on solid, level ground.

Ask the Lord to draw near to those who struggle with assurance, with the promise and guarantee of his redeeming love.

State your case

We've seen God on trial. We've seen the false gods of the nations on trial. Now it's our own turn.

Read Isaiah 43:14-28

❓ *What does God promise (v 14)?*

Verses 16-17 are a description of the parting of the Red Sea. Verse 20 refers to the provision of water for the people in Exodus 15 and 17. Once again, we are reading about a new exodus.

But God goes further in Isaiah 43:18-19. "See, I am doing a new thing!" God is saying, *Never mind the exodus from Egypt; I'm going to do something bigger, something better.*

Humanity on trial

❓ *Who does God turn to accuse in verse 22?*
❓ *What have they failed to do (v 22-23)?*

God's demands are not heavy (v 23); it's the people's actions that are burdensome (v 24). God invites the people to state the case for their innocence (v 26). But they have no hope of proving it.

⌃ Pray

Imagine yourself standing in the dock in this trial. What would you say? It's striking that God's people here can't even be bothered to ask for God's help (v 22). Are there ways in which you may be guilty of the same thing? Are there other ways in which you have failed to honour or serve God (v 23)? Spend some time in confession before the Lord.

The verdict

Re-read Isaiah 43:25

This trial has a twist, and the twist is Jesus. 800 years after Isaiah, John the Baptist saw Jesus and said, "Look, the Lamb of God, who takes away the sin of the world!" (John 1:29). The evidence is presented. The verdict is clear. But Jesus steps in and takes our place. As a result, God "blots out your transgressions ... and remembers your sins no more".

Why does God do this? It's for us. But also for his own sake (Isaiah 43:25)—that is, to reveal his glory and grace.

Read Isaiah 44:1-5

Here's the result of the trial. God will bring his people home. By his Spirit, he will lead us from slavery to sonship.

In the future Jesus will lead us to a new home in a new heaven and a new earth. But already he has led us home to God. If you're in Christ by faith, you can say, "I belong to the LORD" (v 5). You belong in God's family, in God's presence, in God's future. You can kick your shoes off, put your feet on the sofa and feel at home.

⌃ Pray

Use the words of 44:1-5 to help you celebrate what God has done for you in Christ.

Best-laid plans

The book of Isaiah has powerful things to say to us about our spiritual state and why Jesus came. But it also reveals how God worked in history long before Jesus' birth.

❷ *In what situations might people find it particularly hard to trust God?*

❷ *Why do you think it's sometimes hard to understand what God is doing?*

True promises

Read Isaiah 44:24 – 45:13

44:24-26 may seem familiar. We've already seen how God alone can fulfil predictions of the future because only he is "the LORD, the Maker of all things" (see 41:21-27; 43:10-13).

❷ *What specific predictions is God making here (44:26-28)?*

Isaiah is looking ahead to the time when the people's exile in Babylon will end. Babylon will fall to the Persians. The Persian king, Cyrus, and his successors will allow God's people to return. Sure enough, we can now read of this return and the rebuilding of Jerusalem in the books of Ezra and Nehemiah.

❷ *What does God say he will help Cyrus to do (45:1-2)?*

❷ *Why might it be surprising that God uses Cyrus in this way (v 4)?*

❷ *But what does God say will happen as a result (v 6-7)?*

Pot and potter

❷ *Who do you think the "potsherds" of verse 9 represent?*

❷ *What does the clay say to the potter (v 9) and the child to its parents (v 10)?*

❷ *What would be the equivalent things to say to God?*

❷ *What are people saying to God (v 11)?*

Once again we are seeing God's "strange work" (see 28:21). It seemed strange that God sent his people into exile. Now it seems strange that he is using someone who isn't even part of his people to bring them out of exile.

Perhaps this is why Isaiah says, "Truly you are a God who has been hiding himself" (45:15). God's ways are hidden and they seem strange.

Read Isaiah 45:15-19

❷ *What will happen if we trust in God, even if his ways seem strange or hidden?*

⌄ Apply

God does not tell us to seek him in vain (v 19). Jesus promises, "Seek and you will find" (Matthew 7:7).

❷ *How can you seek God today?*

❷ *Are you facing difficult or strange things? How can you express trust in him even when his ways seem hidden to you?*

The fall of Babylon

Today we look at two final passages from Isaiah 40 – 48.

Read Isaiah 47:1-11

Here Babylon, the nation which would take God's people into captivity, is personified as a great queen.

> ❓ *How has God used Babylon (v 6)?*
> ❓ *What lesson do you think Babylon should have learned?*
> ❓ *What has Babylon said about herself (v 7, 8, 10)?*

It's a parody of what God says about himself (see 45:18; 46:5, 9-10). Babylon has grown arrogant. She is putting herself in God's place.

> ❓ *Why does Babylon feel so good about herself (47:1, 5, 8, 10)?*
> ❓ *But what will happen to her (v 1-3, 9, 11)?*

If only

Read Isaiah 48:1-11, 17-22

God used Babylon to chastise his people, but she failed to learn the very lessons she was dispensing. In Isaiah 48, we see how God's people have themselves failed to listen properly.

> ❓ *What did God tell them in the past, and why (v 3-6)?*
> ❓ *How did they respond (v 8)?*
> ❓ *What would have happened if they'd listened properly (v 18-19)?*
> ❓ *What has been the effect on them of the exile (v 10)?*
> ❓ *What will God communicate now (v 6b-7)?*
> ❓ *What should the people do (v 20)?*

⌄ Apply

This picture of Babylon is a warning to those of us today who feel comfortable and secure. Do we feel superior because we are well off or successful? Do we trust in our own wisdom and knowledge and assume that nothing can touch us? We need to recognize that God is the Lord, and there is no other. "Our Redeemer—the LORD Almighty is his name—is the Holy One of Israel" (v 4). We are entirely dependent on him.

⌃ Pray

Ask God to help you to learn the lessons Babylon and Israel failed to learn. Ask him to show you where you are not paying attention to his word, or where you are claiming to be more faithful to him than you really are (v 1-2). Confess your sins and ask for the help of God's Holy Spirit in listening to him and obeying his word more fully in the future. Thank him that in Christ there is forgiveness for when you fail to be faithful.

What's it worth?

One way or another that's a question we often ask. Imagine someone asked that about the cross of Christ. What would you say? In Isaiah 49 we find the true answer.

We've already read one of Isaiah's "servant songs" (42:1-9). Today's passage is another. We're listening in to a dialogue between the LORD and his Servant.

Read Isaiah 49:1-7

❓ *Who is the Servant and what is his job (v 3)?*

Isaiah here was looking ahead to a time when Israel would be in exile in Babylon. Instead of attracting the nations to the ways of the Lord, Israel had been attracted to the ways of the nations. They had failed to honour God's name. This is why the Servant says, "I have laboured in vain; I have spent my strength for nothing at all" (v 4). The land lies desolate, the king is a captive and the temple is in ruins. Israel has failed to be the Servant of the LORD.

A true servant

But in 49:5 the Servant is someone other than Israel, because he is going to gather Israel back to God—and be the light of the world that Israel was supposed to have been. A few hundred years later, the Lord Jesus stood up and declared, "I am the light of the world" (John 8:12). Jesus is the promised true and faithful Servant.

In Isaiah 49:3 the Lord says, "You are my servant, Israel, in whom I will display my splendour", and Jesus perfectly displays the splendour of God (Hebrews 1:3). If you want to know what God is like, look at Jesus. It's

in Jesus that we see the true holiness, grace, wisdom, justice, compassion, power and love of God. God's honour has been brought into question by the defeat of his people (Isaiah 52:3-6), but Jesus, the Servant, will restore God's reputation.

Worth more

To honour the Servant's obedience, God will restore his people Israel (Isaiah 49:5). But that is not enough. "It is too small a thing" (v 6). The cross deserves more and achieves more.

❓ *Why might Jesus' work have appeared to be in vain (v 4)? When was he "despised and abhorred" (v 7)?*
❓ *But what does Isaiah tell us about the Servant's reward (v 4, 7)?*

God's salvation will reach to the ends of the earth. That is what Jesus' obedience is worth.

⌄ Apply

Every step we make in mission is a step towards the moment when people from every nation, tribe, language and tongue bow down before Jesus' throne. It is too small a thing to be concerned just for your family or local community. Christ is worth more than that. The cross of Christ deserves the nations.

❓ *What is one small thing you can do to contribute to God's worldwide mission?*

Watch them come

Much of the time, evangelism seems like hard work. We wonder whether anyone really wants to hear our message. Isaiah 49 gives us the confidence boost we need.

The first part of Isaiah 49 establishes that the obedience of Jesus merits the nations as a reward. The rest of the chapter describes *how* Jesus will receive his reward.

Read Isaiah 49:8-26

Once again Isaiah promises a new exodus. This whole passage is addressed to the "islands" (v 1), which is Isaiah's way of talking about the Gentiles or non-Jews.

> ❓ *What similarities can you spot between this passage and the story of the exodus from Egypt?*

A new people

> ❓ *Where are people coming from (v 12)?*
> ❓ *What will happen when they all reach the promised land (v 19-21)?*

Isaiah is speaking to God's people in exile with their children far from home. For Isaiah's readers in Babylon, that meant the prospect of their children heading home to a renewed homeland—a powerfully evocative idea for any refugee. But Isaiah is looking beyond exile in Babylon to the work of Christ and the mission of the church. So "your children" are God's people, perhaps especially God's people waiting to be gathered into Christ's kingdom—waiting to become God's children in response to the proclamation of the gospel.

> ❓ *How does God think about his children (v 15-16)?*

Not one of God's people gets forgotten or left behind. God's chosen people will respond when they hear the gospel—and be gathered in by God.

> ❓ *How might that influence the way we think about evangelism?*

Vindication

> ❓ *Who will bring these children (v 22-23)?*

We rarely think of governments and authorities nurturing the church! At the moment in the West, Christianity is marginalised. Elsewhere in the world things are much tougher. But one day God's people will be vindicated and every knee will bow before Jesus.

Liberation

> ❓ *How does Isaiah describe the power of Satan to trap people (v 24)?*
> ❓ *Do you ever feel this way about the people around you?*
> ❓ *How does God respond (v 25-26)?*

⌃ Pray

This passage should give us great confidence in God's power and determination to save. Respond by praying for those you know who are not yet Christians. Use the imagery from this passage to help you pray.

A chip off the old block?

Are you similar to your parents? In Isaiah 51 God reminds Israel of their ancestors, Abraham and Sarah.

But the most important thing about them isn't their own characteristics—it's God's.

Wives and children
Read Isaiah 50:1-3

- ❷ With what tone of voice do you imagine the questions in verses 1-2 being said?
- ❷ What is the reason for God's people being sent away—and what isn't the reason?
- ❷ What is scary about this metaphor of a mother being divorced and a child being sent away?
- ❷ What is hopeful about it?

We skip past 50:4-11 for now, but we'll return to it in two studies' time.

Stones in a quarry
Read Isaiah 51:1-3

- ❷ What are the people told to remember about Abraham and Sarah (v 2)?
- ❷ What does this remind them about God?
- ❷ What does it remind them about themselves (v 1)?
- ❷ How do you think those in exile would have felt to hear this—and then to hear the promise in verse 3?

You and me

In the remainder of Isaiah 51, God explains that the salvation he is bringing will last for ever (v 6, 8). People die and the earth wears out, but God's righteousness and salvation will never fail (v 6-8). Ancient monsters representing primordial chaos (and perhaps pointing to Satan and his angels) will be defeated (v 9-10).

We pick up the passage again in verse 12.

Read Isaiah 51:12-16

- ❷ What are human beings like (v 12)?
- ❷ What is God like (v 15-16)?
- ❷ But what does God say about those he has chosen (v 16)?
- ❷ So how should we think about "mere mortals" (v 12) and "the wrath of the oppressor" (v 13)?

⌃ Pray

The New Testament tells us that all who trust in Jesus Christ are Abraham's children (Galatians 3:29). We are those to whom God says, "You are my people" (Isaiah 51:16).

How do you respond to this? Spend some time in prayer and thanksgiving.

Then take some time to pray for those you know of who are living in fear—for any reason. Ask God to remind them of his power (v 13) and to set them free (v 14). Ask him to give them faith like Abraham, who trusted in God's promises.

One thing

The difficulties of Psalm 26 seem to be in the past now, as this song breathes a new-found confidence in God's faithfulness

Nothing can touch me

Read Psalm 27:1-3

> ❓ *What is David confident of (v 1)?*
> ❓ *How does it affect his approach to life?*

David has discovered the liberating effect that entrusting your life into God's hands can bring. He's afraid of nothing, because he knows that God is his stronghold. Paul knew this: he organised a picnic in the middle of a shipwreck (see Acts 27:32-37). The apostles knew this: they stood fearless before the great men of their day with their simple message of faith in Christ (see Acts 5:29-33). Stephen knew this: he asked forgiveness for his persecutors as they murdered him (see Acts 7:54-60).

> ❓ *Do you have the same liberating confidence in God's sovereign love?*
> ❓ *If not, why do you think that is?*

Desiring God

Read Psalm 27:4-6

When we feel unsafe, our natural instinct is to run to wherever we call "home".

> ❓ *Where is David's "home"?*
> ❓ *Where is yours?*

For David, "home" is the temple—where God lived in the middle of his people.

> ❓ *Why is David so desperate to be with God in verses 4-6?*

The key to his confidence is that he desires God. He wants to be with God more than anything else in the world. David is in love with him, and, of the many things he could ask God for, like Mary (see Luke 10:38-42), there's only one thing David really wants—to be with him.

☑ Apply

This is not some kind of religious fervour that we can work up in ourselves. It's the result of understanding the truth, and being ruthless with the alternatives. So how do you score on this quick test of how much you love God: which of these options would you prefer:

- To talk to God in prayer, or to talk to friends on the phone?
- To read the Bible, or to watch TV?
- To be with other believers, or to be with other friends?
- To be in heaven with him, or to enjoy life on earth?

Holding on

Read Psalm 27:7-14

David's love for God isn't unrealistic. He knows that the problems are real (v 12).

> ❓ *So what keeps David going? What does he tell himself to do (v 14)?*
> ❓ *What do you think that means for you?*

Daughter Zion

If your city or nation were depicted as a male or female figure, what do you think their character would be like?

Read Isaiah 51:17-23

As in 50:1, God's people are being personified—and it's not a flattering portrait.

- ❷ *Jerusalem is drunk and staggering—but what has she drunk (51:17, 21)?*
- ❷ *How have her children (the people) failed her (v 18-20)?*
- ❷ *How does she feel (v 19)?*

The cup of God's wrath is a picture of receiving his judgment. But now God is going to take away this cup. "Awake, awake!" he cries (v 17). The people are no longer captive and no longer in a drunken sleep.

···· TIME OUT ····

Read Mark 10:38 and 14:32-36

God's promise in Isaiah 51:22 was partially fulfilled when the Jews had spent 70 years in captivity in Babylon. But it was ultimately fulfilled when Jesus took God's judgment in our place. He drank the cup of wrath fully so that now there is no wrath left for us.

Awake, awake!
Read Isaiah 52:1-12

- ❷ *How has the personified Jerusalem changed now (v 1-3)?*
- ❷ *Why was she "sold" (look back at 50:1)?*
- ❷ *What does this "selling" actually mean (52:4)?*

Now Jerusalem will be "redeemed" or bought back—not with money but with the blood of the Saviour (as we'll discover in the following chapter).

- ❷ *What are God's people called to do now that they are free (v 1)?*
- ❷ *What else are they able to do (v 7-9)?*
- ❷ *Why do you think Isaiah describes this as "beautiful" (v 7)?*

⌃ Pray

Spend some time praising God for the way he redeems and rescues, and praying for those you know who do not yet believe.

⌄ Apply

- ❷ *In what ways can people today "bring good news ... proclaim peace ... bring good tidings ... [and] proclaim salvation"?*
- ❷ *Again, practically, what does it mean to say to people, "God reigns!"?*
- ❷ *How can you embody this message in the way you live?*
- ❷ *Who could you share this message with verbally this week?*

Shame and glory

We back-pedal now for a last look at Isaiah 50—which leads us into one of Isaiah's most famous passages.

We have seen repeatedly how God's people have failed to be faithful. Time for another portrait of the Servant who *was* faithful.

Read Isaiah 50:4-9

❷ *What is the relationship like between the Servant and the* LORD?

❷ *When the Servant listens, what does he hear (v 4)?*

❷ *Why (v 5)?*

❷ *But what has happened—how have people treated the Servant (v 6)?*

Shame and spitting

Re-read Isaiah 50:1 and 51:17-23

❷ *What disgrace have God's people experienced? Why?*

The Servant also experiences mockery—but he says, "I will not be disgraced" (50:7).

❷ *Why not (v 8-9)?*

❷ *How does he show his confidence in God's vindication (51:7-9)?*

Marred and disfigured

Read Isaiah 52:13-15

These verses lead up to what is perhaps the most famous passage in the book of Isaiah and one of the most famous passages in the entire Old Testament—Isaiah 53, the fourth and final "servant song". This introductory stanza contains hints of the climax of the song, which we'll look at tomorrow.

❷ *How does 50:4-9 help us to understand what it means that the Servant "will act wisely" and "be raised and lifted up" (52:13)?*

❷ *How does 52:14 help us to understand why the Servant is mocked and spat at (50:6)?*

Think of Jesus hanging on the cross. The whips have pulled away his flesh until his bone is exposed. The crown of thorns has sent trickles of blood down his face. His weakened frame has collapsed under the weight of the cross. His face is harrowed by the inner anguish of his soul. As a result, he looks less than human.

Yet God raised Jesus from the dead and exalted him to the highest place.

Salvation

In Isaiah 6:9 we learned that Isaiah's message would be preached to those who would hear, but not understand. But now that message kicks into reverse. People who have not heard will understand (52:15). People who never knew about God at all will be saved.

⌃ Pray

Praise God for Jesus—who endured disgrace, not because of his own sins, but because of ours, and who was raised to life for our salvation (Romans 4:25).

By his wounds

We've heard a lot about the faithful Servant who would redeem God's people. But how? Isaiah 53 makes it clear at last.

Read Isaiah 53:1-12

The song is in five stanzas or sections. We already read the first stanza in Isaiah 52:13-15.

❓ *What would you say is the main theme of the second stanza (53:1-3)?*

Jesus was a human being just like any of us. There seemed to be nothing special about him. People despised him for it. They hung him on the cross, and the sight was so appalling that people hid their faces (v 3).

❓ *Why does it seem so unbelievable (v 1) that God's Servant should be like this?*

Substitution

It looks like Jesus is being punished by God (v 4). But right at the heart of this song is this amazing truth: while it is true that Jesus is being punished by God, it is not for his sins but for ours (v 4-6).

❓ *How many times does Isaiah use the word "our" in these verses?*
❓ *What overall impression do you get of what we are like?*
❓ *What do we gain because of Jesus' suffering?*

The act these verses describe is the centrepiece of the Bible story, of our salvation, of the course of human history, of the hope of God's people. Everything turns on Jesus' amazing act of substitution at the cross.

Like a lamb

❓ *What do verses 7-9 show about what the servant is like?*

Humanly speaking, Jesus' death was a blatant act of injustice. But in verse 10 it turns out it was the Lord's will—and therefore an act of perfect justice. Jesus wasn't taken unawares—this was the plan he and the Father made together, from the beginning (v 10). The resurrection is the glorious sign that the plan has worked and that justice has been served: our sins have been fully dealt with, and the innocent Jesus returns to life.

❓ *In what ways will the Servant be rewarded (v 10-12)?*
❓ *Why is Jesus' death on the cross an act of justice?*

⌃ Pray

Read Isaiah 53 again.

❓ *What does each part of this passage tell you about yourself?*
❓ *What does it tell you about God?*

Spend time responding in prayer—confessing your sins and worshipping Jesus.

The great reward

Human beings don't get a good write-up in Isaiah 53. We're sinners, transgressors, rejecters. But look more closely and you start to see yourself in a different way altogether.

Read Isaiah 52:13-15 and 53:10-12

At the end, the song circles back to where it started. Jesus is vindicated—"raised and lifted up and highly exalted" (52:13). He takes his seat on his throne at the right hand of the Father (Hebrews 1:3). He is victorious.

The result? The justification of many.

❷ *Who are the "many" in Isaiah 52:13-15 and 53:10-12?*
❷ *What do the "many" do? What happens to them?*

Sprinkling in Isaiah 52:15 is an act of purification (see Numbers 8:6-7). It means being saved and cleansed from sin.

Jesus' portion

The word "great" in Isaiah 53:12 is a bit misleading. While the word can mean "great", it can also mean "many" or "numerous" (Exodus 1:7). That is what it has meant so far in this song. So this is not about the Servant cosying up to the great and the good. The "many" are "his offspring" and those whom he has justified (Isaiah 53:10-11). It also helps to realise that the words "give", "portion" and "divide" are all the same word in Hebrew. Put this all together and we get this more literal translation of verse 12:

"Therefore I will allocate many
    as an allocation to him
and he will allocate the strong as plunder."

God does the allocating in the first half; the Servant's reward is us: God's people—you and me. God gives many people to Jesus.

Our portion

The Servant does the allocating in the second half of the verse. Just like a triumphant king distributing the fruit of his success among his loyal retainers, Jesus distributes the rewards of his success among his people. Jesus invites us to share his victory.

What's our reward? At the moment we're besieged and beset by the world around us. In the West we're mocked and marginalised. Elsewhere in the world Christians are persecuted and imprisoned. But the strong don't win. We win! In fact, we've already won because Jesus has risen from the dead. The enemies of God did their worst, and it was not enough to overcome Jesus. They can do their worst to us, but nothing will separate us from the love of Christ (Romans 8:35-39).

⌃ Pray

❷ *What impact does it have on you to see that you are not just part of the reason for the cross, but also part of Jesus' reward for his suffering?*

Ask God to help you see yourself in the way he sees you. Pray for others too who may need to hear this message.

A city and a bride

What makes you feel beautiful, strong, secure or peaceful?

Read Isaiah 54:1-17

Chapters 54 – 55 extend the idea of the "many" who are made Jesus' "offspring". In 54:1 Isaiah calls on a barren woman to sing because she is about to bear many children. It's a picture of God's barren people about to see many converts.

❓ *Why do you think God uses the image of a woman who has never had children? How does this image make you feel?*
❓ *What will God's people need to do (v 2)?*

My beloved

In verses 4-10 the metaphor of the barren woman is developed. Now God is addressing his people as his wife.

❓ *What is the history of this wife and husband (v 6-8)?*
❓ *What does that correspond to in the history of God's people?*
❓ *But what does God promise his bride (v 4, 6, 8, 9-10)?*
❓ *How can God's people be sure that he will keep this promise (v 9)?*

A city of turquoise

Now the metaphor changes and God's people are described as a city.

❓ *Where do we see the following themes in verses 11-17?*
  • *Security*
  • *Beauty*
  • *Peace*

···· TIME OUT ··

Read Revelation 21:1-4, 9-11, 18-21, 22-27

❓ *How does the writer of Revelation pick up these same images and themes?*
❓ *What new promises are added?*

This passage in Revelation is describing our future. The church is God's bride, the Holy City. The promises which God makes to his people in Isaiah 54 are also promises to us today. Jesus is preparing us as his bride to live with him for ever—and no one can take us away from him.

⌄ Apply

❓ *How do you respond to this idea of being God's bride? Does it make you see yourself any differently? Does it make you see God any differently?*
❓ *Is there anything you feel ashamed about? How does this passage help you not to be ashamed?*
❓ *Is there anything you feel afraid of? How does this passage help you not to be afraid?*

Come to the waters

It's not just you and me. One day the whole of creation will be joining in with God's redemption plan.

Jesus took "the punishment that brought us peace" (Isaiah 53:5). In Isaiah 55 we see even more about what Jesus' death achieved—and it's joyful.

Read Isaiah 55:1-2

> ❷ *What invitation goes out (v 1)?*
> ❷ *What is special about this purchase (v 1)?*
> ❷ *What's the alternative thing to buy (v 2)?*

True satisfaction

Isaiah is calling us to turn from our empty, unsatisfying ways and find true satisfaction in God.

> ❷ *What things do you think people today seek satisfaction in? Why?*
> ❷ *How long do those things last?*

Read Isaiah 55:3-13

> ❷ *What promises does God make (v 3-7, 12-13)?*
> ❷ *Compare those things to other potential sources of satisfaction. Why is God more satisfying than anything else?*

This is the call that comes to us today in the gospel. Jesus has paid the price for sin. Now we can freely take God's gifts to us, without cost. It's not just water, wine, milk and bread—it's life itself he offers us (v 3). He even promises to endow us with splendour so that people from all across the world will come running to us. As a result of Jesus' sacrificial death and resurrection, we can now represent his rule in such a way that it attracts those who aren't yet part of God's people.

Fruitful words

Re-read Isaiah 55:8-11

> ❷ *What is special about God's ways and thoughts?*
> ❷ *In what way are God's words like snow or rain (v 10)?*
> ❷ *How does this help us to trust in him?*
> ❷ *How does this link to the theme of satisfaction we saw earlier in this chapter?*

Joy for ever

Re-read Isaiah 55:12-13

There is so much joy in the redemption of humanity that even the created world will be caught up in it. This is the kind of world we are part of, thanks to Jesus—a world of joy, peace, and singing; a world of fruitfulness instead of hard thorns.

⌄ Apply

> ❷ *Where do you tend to look for joy, peace, or satisfaction?*
> ❷ *What do you think it looks like to find those things in Jesus instead?*
> ❷ *What can you do practically to help yourself seek those things in him?*

The prayers of faith

There are two prayers in this psalm that are intimately linked together. Let's get to grips with the first before we see how it produces the second.

Read Psalm 28:1-5

Real praying

❷ *What is David's worry (v 1-2)?*

❷ *What's his remarkably honest plea (v 3-5)?*

❷ *But what is God most concerned with (v 5a)?*

It's easy to read the way David calls down judgment on his enemies as sheer vindictiveness, but that is to misunderstand it completely. David is the Lord's anointed one. So opposition to him is by definition opposition to the living God. And verse 4 outlines the basis of his call for judgment: it is what they deserve for their acts of evil.

⌄ Apply

We often have to deal with frustrating people who seem to be out to wreck our purposes—whether that's the garage badly repairing your car, or those people at church who seem to hold back progress.

❷ *In what circumstances might it be legitimate to pray about them as David does in verses 4-5?*

Just leave it

Read Psalm 28:6-9

❷ *What is David absolutely convinced of (v 6)?*

❷ *So what is the nature of his prayer now?*

❷ *And how exactly does he feel now? How would you describe his mood?*

You've heard of a prayer of faith. This is a praise of faith. David's circumstances may not have changed—the smiling, polite, but malicious enemies of verse 3 are still there—but he praises God in trust that, having committed the matter to him, God will deal with it.

⌃ Pray

In practice, we find it less easy to "leave things with the Lord". But continued worry about things we have prayed over can just be faithlessness in the power, intention and sovereignty of the living Lord, who holds both you and all evildoers in his hand.

Spend some time now in prayer for those who oppose the gospel.

Encourage yourself with the truth of verse 5, then—well, *you know what to do, don't you?*

A call to justice

What words would you use to describe your church? What values does it uphold?

In chapters 40 – 55 Isaiah looked ahead to the time when Babylon would enslave God's people. Isaiah promised freedom, but his vision of salvation looked beyond liberation from Babylon to liberation from sin and death through Jesus. In chapters 56 – 66 Isaiah looks ahead to the return of the Jews to Judea to reconstruct their country, which took place under Ezra and Nehemiah. But again Isaiah also looks beyond the return from exile. These chapters are a promise of a worldwide church created through a worldwide mission.

A covenant community
Read Isaiah 56:1-2

❓ *What should characterise God's people?*

Read Isaiah 56:3-8

Not only could eunuchs not have children, they were also barred from entering the temple—as were foreigners.

❓ *What might foreigners and eunuchs say (v 3)?*
❓ *But what does God promise them now (v 4-7)?*
❓ *Again, what is involved in being part of God's covenant people?*

Dream v reality

But this is not how things were in Isaiah's day.

Read Isaiah 56:9 – 57:13

❓ *In these verses, how do we see people failing to...*
  • *maintain justice (see 56:1)?*
  • *choose what pleases God (see v 4)?*
  • *bind themselves to the Lord and love his name (see v 6)?*

An offer of peace
Read Isaiah 57:14-21

❓ *How is God described in verse 15?*
❓ *What is his attitude towards the people who have been described in the preceding verses (v 16-18)?*
❓ *What kind of person does he welcome (v 15)?*
❓ *But what does he say about those who continue to reject him (v 20-21)?*

⌃ Pray

❓ *Where do you see injustice in the communities around you?*
❓ *In what ways have you been involved in causing injustice yourself?*
❓ *How do you think your church is doing at being the community of justice God desires?*

God offers you peace. Ask him to give you a contrite heart (v 15). Ask him to help you and your church to live up to the description of his covenant community in 56:1-8.

Land of darkness

If you could get to a vantage point over the community where you live and look over it, what would you see?

Looking with spiritual eyes, you'd probably see deep spiritual darkness. That's what God saw when he looked at his people in Isaiah's time.

Read Isaiah 58:1-14

The people complain that God is ignoring their religious performances (v 1-3).

> ❷ *What's the answer—why is God unimpressed with their fasting (v 3-5)?*
> ❷ *What does he demand instead (v 6-7)?*

God's people need to do justice—then they will be a light to the nations (v 8, 10). Then they will be blessed by God (v 9, 11-12, 14).

> ❷ *What do images like "dawn", "light" and "the noonday" conjure up in your mind?*

But darkness is what God sees when he looks at his people, not light. As a result they have separated themselves from him—as Isaiah 59:1-3 explains. When God looks across the land, he sees only injustice.

Like the blind

Read Isaiah 59:9-15

In verses 9-11 Isaiah expresses what it feels like to live in this unjust world.

> ❷ *Have you ever felt like this? Why?*
> ❷ *Who else do you know who feels this way?*

But it will come as no surprise when Isaiah acknowledges the cause of this injustice, darkness and despair.

> ❷ *Whose fault is it (v 12-13)?*

You might be expecting Isaiah to talk about God sending his people into exile at this point. After all, that's often what Isaiah does after pointing out the people's sinfulness.

But in this part of Isaiah, we are looking further ahead.

Read Isaiah 59:16-21

The Lord sees that there is no one to intervene. So he himself intervenes. Isaiah pictures God as a warrior, putting on armour to fight for justice.

> ❷ *Who will he attack (v 18-19)?*
> ❷ *Who will he save (v 20)?*
> ❷ *How will he ultimately guarantee a renewal of justice among his people (v 21)?*

✔ Apply

Today we are living in the time of the new covenant which God promised in verse 21. If we trust in Christ, his Spirit will not depart from us. Doing justice and bringing light to a dark world is now our calling.

Look back through Isaiah 58 – 59.

> ❷ *Is there a particular instance of justice or injustice that strikes a chord with you?*
> ❷ *What action could you take to bring light to these types of situation today?*

The light of the world

Darkness covers the earth. Humanity is groping in the dark, looking for answers. But light has come!

❷ *In what senses do you think people around you are walking in darkness?*

❷ *What would it look like for light to burst into those situations?*

Read Isaiah 60:1-4

❷ *What is the light that has come (v 1, 2)?*

Back in 9:2 Isaiah had said, "The people walking in darkness have seen a great light; on those living in the land of deep darkness a light has dawned". Light is coming because "a child is born ... a son is given" (9:6). God is coming in the person of his Son to bring light.

Jesus said, "I am the light of the world. Whoever follows me will never walk in darkness, but will have the light of life" (John 8:12).

❷ *What difference do you think knowing Jesus would make to the situations you thought of earlier?*

You will be radiant

Read Isaiah 60:5

What is the impact on God's people? "Then you will look and be radiant". Light shines on us, and as a result we light up! We radiate, reflecting the glory of Jesus.

❷ *How else does Isaiah describe how those who see Jesus feel?*

❷ *Why do you think that makes them "radiant"?*

❷ *Who do they radiate light to (v 3, 5)?*

TIME OUT

Chapters 40 – 55 are full of references to the Servant of the Lord. All the time there is one Servant. But after Isaiah has described the Servant's work of salvation through suffering, that changes (see 54:17; 65:9, 14). Through the work of Jesus, we all become God's servants.

It's not just that Israel will be a light to the nations, but people from the nations will be a light to the nations. That's what's happening in Isaiah 60:4. Isaiah wants us to lift up our eyes and see people flooding into the church around the world.

Read Isaiah 60:6-16

❷ *How does the radiance of God's people result in him being honoured?*

✔ Apply

We are the fulfilment of Isaiah's vision. The nations come to Jerusalem to discover God's ways. But they don't come to geographic Jerusalem; they come to spiritual Jerusalem— to the church scattered across the globe.

What's the application? "Arise, shine, for your light has come" (v :1). Walk in the light; keep your eyes fixed on God; shine with his light. Do good deeds that bring glory to your Father.

A new sun

What do you imagine when you think of the new creation?

Isaiah has said our light will come. We've seen how this happens in the person of Christ. As a result, the church becomes a light to the world, and the nations join God's people. It's all so exciting. But Isaiah keeps on going. There's no stopping him. There'll be so much light, he says, we won't even need the sun!

Read Isaiah 60:17-22

Isaiah is not getting carried away with his rhetoric. He is moving beyond this world and into the next world.

> ❷ *What else does Isaiah promise?*
> ❷ *Do you believe this?*

This is where our witness to the world leads. Your light may seem dim. The darkness may sometimes feel overwhelming. But this is the outcome. One day our witness—your witness—will result in a city of light with people from every nation. However small we seem, our contribution matters—and the triumph of the gospel is certain (v 22).

Pray

Spend time reflecting on this vision of the future. Ask God to make this kingdom come, on earth as in heaven!

Culture matters

Revelation 21:23-26 picks up the imagery of Isaiah 60 in the way it describes the new Jerusalem—the future of God's people. Revelation 21:25 says that this city's gates will never be shut. This idea is taken from Isaiah 60:11-12.

Read Isaiah 60:6-16

> ❷ *Why won't the gates be shut (v 11)?*

These verses are an inventory of the world's wealth being brought to God's people. All that is good in the economies and cultures of the nations will find a place in the new Jerusalem (Revelation 21:24-26). This vision of the climax of history gives great value to what we do *in* history. There seems to be some measure of cultural continuity between this age and the next. Human cultures are not trashed at the end of history; they are fulfilled.

This means culture matters. As we seek to go to the nations, we must celebrate that we are all one in Christ Jesus—yet be careful not to impose our own cultural norms on others. In our churches, we should express both our unity in the gospel across cultures and the value of cultural diversity and local cultural expression.

Apply

> ❷ *How do you think you could put this into practice in your church?*

Present and future

Which of Isaiah's promises do we experience now—and which should we still be waiting for? It sometimes gets confusing.

Read Isaiah 61:1-3

Here God's servant is anointed by God's Spirit to proclaim good news. It's a passage that Jesus applies to himself in Luke 4:16-21.

❓ *Who did Jesus come for?*
❓ *What changes does he bring?*

Read Isaiah 62:1-12

❓ *What changes do we see in verses 2-4?*

God will "marry" the land, removing her shame for ever. It is a promise fulfilled as Jesus dies to beautify his bride (Ephesians 5:25-27).

God will come to dwell in Jerusalem, which will therefore be known as "the City No Longer Deserted" (Isaiah 62:10-12). It is a promise partially fulfilled in the presence of the Spirit in the church, and fully fulfilled in the new Jerusalem, which is described as a bride and of which it is said, "Look! God's dwelling-place is now among the people, and he will dwell with them" (Revelation 21:2-3).

Two ages

Once again, Isaiah is looking beyond this world and into the next world. Or, perhaps more accurately, he just sees the future. It's us who can now recognise that the new age began with the resurrection of Jesus but is not yet fulfilled. We can see that Isaiah's

vision of the future in fact happens in two stages: with the first and second comings of Jesus. This is why it is not always clear which elements of Isaiah's vision belong to which phase.

Of course, these two ages overlap. The old age of darkness still continues, but the new age of light has already dawned. What we as followers of Christ experience in history is a foretaste of the coming age.

Look back over Isaiah 61:1-3 and 62:1-12 (and read the remainder of chapter 61 if you have time).

❓ *Which of these things do we experience now?*
❓ *Which are we still waiting for?*
❓ *Is there anything here which you know can be experienced now, but which you yourself have not experienced?*

🔼 Pray

This passage is a call to prayer. "You who call on the LORD, give yourselves no rest, and give him no rest till he establishes Jerusalem and makes her the praise of the earth" (62:6-7).

Reflecting on this passage, pray for the fulfilment of these promises here on earth.

Tearing the heavens

What creates a praying church or a praying person? What sustains an energy for prayer? It's the recognition of deep need.

Isaiah 63 – 64 shows us what it looks like to pray with deep passion.

In chapter 63, God is described as a warrior coming to judge (v 1-6). Isaiah then recalls the story of the first exodus from Egypt (v 7-14) and makes this the basis of a prayer asking that God will again liberate his people.

Read Isaiah 63:15 – 64:12

❷ *What problems does Isaiah identify (63:15-19)?*
❷ *What does he long for God to do (63:15; 64:1, 9)?*

Isaiah is looking ahead. In 64:10-11 he says Jerusalem is "a desolation" and the temple "has been burned with fire". When Isaiah himself speaks, that hasn't happened yet. It would be another two centuries before Jerusalem would be destroyed. But Isaiah has predicted it, and now he imagines what it will be like for the returning exiles. He prays with passion because he foresees their need.

A problem

If we were just looking at a contest between Israel and the nations, 64:1-4 would make perfect sense. Israel is in trouble. God is on Israel's side. So Isaiah asks God to fight against the nations. Job done (v 3)!

❷ *But what's the problem (v 5-7)?*
❷ *What position does that put Israel in?*

Isaiah's already spotted this problem. In 63:10 he said that because of the people's rebellion, "[God] turned and became their enemy".

The battle that really matters isn't Israel versus the nations but humanity versus God. There's nothing we can do to clean up our act (64:6). How can we be saved (v 5)?

God comes down

Read Mark 1:10

❷ *What link can you spot with Isaiah 64:1?*

God has come to us in the person of his Son. The baptism of Jesus was the moment when God responded to Isaiah's plea, as God tore the heavens open and the Spirit came down to anoint his Son.

❷ *What is the answer, therefore, to Isaiah's questions in verses 5 and 12?*

⌃ Pray

What needs do you see in the world around you? Where do you wish God would tear the heavens and come down to sort things out?

Praise him that he has already sent his Son to guarantee the restoration of all things.

Ask him to intervene now—and to show you how he could work through you to help meet others' needs.

A double ending

Don't miss the grandeur of what Isaiah promises at the climax of his book.

Read Isaiah 65:17-25

"See, I will create new heavens and a new earth", says God in verse 17.

> ❓ *Where in this passage do you see the following things?*
> - *Joy*
> - *Safety*
> - *Abundance*
> - *Divine help*
> - *Peace*

Take a moment to think what a contrast this is to the threats and fears of the present age.

The one exception to this picture of universal harmony is the serpent, who will eat dust (v 25)—an allusion to the defeat of Satan (Genesis 3:14-15).

Two futures

Read Isaiah 66:1-24

> ❓ *What two futures does Isaiah describe in verses 2-6 and 7-13?*
> ❓ *Who will experience them?*

⌄ Apply

As we read verse 2, it is worth pausing to ask what our own attitude is to God's word. It is so easy to listen to a sermon and evaluate the preacher. Or we can sit there considering how the message applies to those around us. God blesses those who are eager to hear God's voice, humble enough

to repent as their sin is exposed and ready to obey what God calls them to do.

A new world

> ❓ *What is involved in Isaiah's final vision of the new creation (v 18-23)?*

Imagine yourself in this new world which Isaiah has been describing.

> ❓ *What is it like? What do you see and hear? What are you most looking forward to about it?*

But there is another ending too (v 24).

Both these endings are coming. The question is: which one will be yours? The answer turns on your attitude to God and his word. It's not that you have to be perfect and do all the right things. God knows we are frail and sinful, and he is patient with us. But we must humble ourselves in contrition. Then God will favour us with a place in the new creation.

⌃ Pray

Humble yourself before God—recognising that you can bring him nothing (v 1-2). Ask him to look after you as a mother looks after a child (v 13). Ask him to bring about what he has promised. Ask him to make you part of this wonderful new world. Pray for loved ones who don't yet know him—that the new creation would be their destination too.

LUKE: Mercy sermon

Jesus is halfway through his sermon on the plain. He has called a new Israel—12 disciples instead of 12 tribes. He has preached a new, deeper law.

And he has called for a mindset of mercy that reflects the mercy that God has shown to us.

Why mercy matters

Read Luke 6:32-36

- ❓ *What is Jesus' repeated question in verses 32, 33 and 34?*
- ❓ *Why does mercy matter? What reasons can you see in the passage?*
- ❓ *What will we get in return for being merciful (v 35)?*
- ❓ *Do you find the use of "credit" and "reward" a surprise? Why or why not?*

This passage raises two important questions. *Is Jesus talking about a sort of contract?* It sounds as if we get "credit" with God for being merciful and as a result he makes us into his sons (v 35). But the rest of the Bible is clear—we are saved by grace. We cannot earn our salvation. And secondly, *is Jesus saying that we should be out for what we can get?* If we are being merciful for the sake of a reward, isn't that just another way of being selfish? But there is more to these statements than is at first apparent.

The reward of mercy

- ❓ *What relationship to God do the disciples already have (v 36)?*
- ❓ *Yet what must they learn to "be"?*

Christians are already God's children in

status, but we also need to *become* his children (i.e. become like him) in practice. Jesus says that if we love our enemies, our great reward is to become like God, who is "kind to the ungrateful and wicked". It's not some sort of contract or way of earning God's favour. Jesus is just saying that if we walk in God's ways, we'll become more like him. The old saying goes like this: "Sow an action, reap a habit; sow a habit, reap a character"—and to have a character like God is a great reward.

The reward for godliness

Re-read Luke 6:32-34

The word "credit", found in some translations, actually means God's favour or "God's smile". Jesus' point is that if we walk on God's path (the path of a mercy-filled life) we will find it leads to a great reward: God himself—and his favour. Not some bag of special goodies that God will give us for being good. But the reward of being with him—now and in heaven, knowing his smile for ever.

⌄ Apply

- ❓ *Which of these reasons do you struggle most with?*
- ❓ *Which of them most motivates you?*

Turn your responses into prayer.

Bible in a year: 2 Kings 4 – 6 • Matthew 12:24-50

Two ways to reject

Jesus has been talking about how we relate to a world that rejects God. The problem is that we can easily slip into rejecting God ourselves in a more subtle way.

Read Luke 6:35-37

We're still talking about mercy (look at v 36) and in today's verses, we see two ways of rejecting God's mercy (v 35, 37).

❓ *What are they?*

1. Ingratitude and wickedness

It is possible to reject God's mercy by being ungrateful and wicked (v 35). You only have to look back to verses 24-26, where Jesus speaks of "woe" to those who persist in rejecting God. It is possible to miss out on God's mercy.

⌄ Apply

Jesus' test seems to be one of cause and effect. You can tell if the cause is there by the presence of the effect. If I am ungrateful, then it is a clear sign that I have not received God's mercy.

How about what is called "presumptuous sins"? *I can do that because I know he'll let me off. After all, Jesus died for me...* Doesn't that qualify as ungrateful and wicked?

If that was the pattern of my life you ought to describe me as a non-Christian.

❓ *Do you ever find yourself thinking that way?*

2. Judgmentalism

Re-read Luke 6:37

❓ *If I judge and condemn others what will happen to me?*
❓ *Why?*

I will be judged and condemned if I am judgmental and condemning. Why? Because I see myself sitting on the judge's bench rather than standing in the dock (v 37). I give my advice to God. I point the finger at others. I don't doubt that God will accept me. But that's tragic. If I think I am a judge, I won't ever ask for mercy or forgiveness.

···· TIME OUT ····

Read Luke 15:11-32

The Bible highlights two ways of rejecting God and his mercy—irreligious and religious. The two sons stand for these two ways. The particular problem with the religious form of rejection is that it is so subtle—we do not see that we are rejecting God.

⌃ Pray

How about a reality check? Is there anyone about whom you feel in your heart, "God should really punish him/her"? Hopefully, the answer is "no one". Ask God to rescue you from ingratitude, smug complacency and judgmentalism.

Judging and judging…

Ok, we should not judge—but there's another angle to consider. Jesus' ban on judgmentalism is often used to suggest that we shouldn't label anything as wrong.

People believe it's judgmental to say, for example, that homosexual sex or abortion is wrong—after all, we are all sinners in different ways.

Read Luke 6:37

Have a look at what Jesus actually says in the round:

❷ *Is there such a thing as wickedness (v 35)?*
❷ *Is forgiveness necessary (v 37)?*
❷ *Are all things equally good (v 43)?*
❷ *Are we supposed to be able to tell what is good or bad (v 42-45)?*

Jesus clearly expects us to judge right from wrong—in fact, ultimately, we should be prepared to help our brother out of sin (v 42). And that is the difference. The judgmental person looks at another's sin from above (from the judge's bench) and condemns. The godly person stands alongside a fellow sinner and tries to help them out.

···· TIME OUT ···

Check out James 5:16 and 1 John 5:16. And let's remember that "there, but for the grace of God, go I".

The rest of Scripture

Read Galatians 6:1

Along with sympathy for the sinner must go hatred of sin—not just "love the sinner and not the sin" but "love the sinner and *hate* the sin"—and hate the sin in ourselves too and

beware of its potent power to corrupt us. Here's the challenge—to judge well about sin without sitting "in judgment" on the sinner.

How can we do it in practice? First, we need to be clear about the difference between God and ourselves (Luke 6:37). He alone is the Judge. We'll think more about this tomorrow. But second, we need to be clear about salvation (v 37, 42). Having tasted God's mercy, we should long for others to taste it too. Think of the difference between someone who longs for sinners to get out of their sin, and someone who simply castigates and despises the sinner. Again, in the parable of the lost sons, the open arms of the Father should be the pattern for us.

⌄ Apply

❷ *What sins do you particularly loathe (clue: it's the ones that really make you angry)?*

Is it the graffiti painters, or the alcoholics; careless drivers or the lawless revellers that plague our town centres these days?

❷ *How are you showing love for those sinners?*
❷ *Which sinners do you particularly love? Are you ignoring their sin?*
❷ *Do you need to make an effort to help them out of it?*

The imitation of God

We're spending a lot of time on this short section, because it is so important for how we conduct ourselves as believers in a world filled with sin.

Read Luke 6:36-37

> ❷ *In what way are we supposed to imitate God? And in what way are we not?*
> ❷ *Do you find it hard to draw this line in real life?*

We are to be merciful because that is what God is like (v 36). We are not to judge others because that is God's role (v 37). The difference is between God's character and his role. True godliness means imitating his character but not imitating his role.

The problem

It's very easy to get this the wrong way round—acting as God rather than following God. And it's a particular problem for religious people. Notice that Jesus is not talking to the irreligious. As committed Christians, we think, know and talk a great deal about God—what a clever trick of Satan to get us to slip into behaving as if we are God!

⌄ Apply

> ❷ *Is it possible to be right—but in the wrong way?*

For example:

- right about a point of doctrine, but dismissive of those who differ.
- working flat out in church service and ministry, but looking down on those who seem to be "slacking".

- praying a lot, but questioning the faith of those not often at the prayer meeting.

> ❷ *Can you add any examples?*

The solution

Re-read Luke 6:36-37

Have you noticed a common theme in the last few studies? The need to see God as he really is, and ourselves as we really are.

···· TIME OUT ····

Read Isaiah 6:1-8

Isaiah saw the holiness and glory of the Lord (v 1-4). Isaiah saw his own sin and how he was polluted along with those around him (v 5). Isaiah received mercy (v 6-7). As a forgiven sinner, Isaiah was sent out (v 8). We find exactly the same pattern with the apostle Paul (1 Timothy 1:15-17).

⌃ Pray

Dear Father, please show me yourself in such a way that I may never again be tempted to act as God. Show me your glory. Show me my own sin. Show me your amazing mercy. Please show me and keep showing me and so fill my heart with the wonder of your goodness to me. Please show me so that I cannot help showing mercy to others, and telling others of your mercy. In Jesus' name, Amen.

The priority of forgiveness

"It is in pardoning that we are pardoned"—so goes the song based on a prayer of Francis of Assisi. But what does that mean?

Read Luke 6:37; Matthew 18:21-35

❷ *What is the big shock in this parable?*

❷ *What is the big point that Jesus is making?*

In the parable, the king pardons his servant before the servant's attitude is put to the test (Matthew 18:27). The shock is that the forgiven servant *will not* forgive. From the New Testament we know that we pardon others because we have already been pardoned. We don't forgive others first, and then impress God into forgiving us.

❷ *And yet—which seems to come first in Luke 6:37?*

❷ *Why does Jesus seem to suggest that forgiving others comes before being forgiven?*

Don't ignore the way the Lord expresses things here or we'll miss the other side of the forgiveness coin. *We cannot be forgiven without becoming forgivers!* We cannot become Christians and receive mercy without becoming "mercy people". The world wants revenge and requires payback, but joining the Christian counter-culture involves ditching the payback mentality and embracing pardon.

That's why the unforgiving servant ends up not being forgiven at all (look again at Matthew 18:32-34). That is the point which Jesus makes in verse 35 and in Luke 6:37. Being forgiving is not an optional add-on for the Christian, but so much part of discipleship

that Jesus says it is necessary to forgive if we are to be forgiven.

⌃ Pray

This can be so difficult—partly because it is often painful to forgive those who have really hurt us, partly because we find it hard to tell whether or not we really are forgiving them (more on that tomorrow). But for now...

- praise God again for his free forgiveness in Jesus.
- pray that we will really see how much more he has forgiven us than we will ever have to forgive in others.

⌄ Apply

Start thinking about people, past and present, Christian or not, whom you need to forgive, and how you might go about putting that forgiveness into practice.

The way to forgive

Forgiveness is easy to talk about in principle, but as the cross shows, in practice it is hard and costly. What does forgiveness look like in practice? What does Scripture say?

How to be forgiving

Read Luke 6:37; Matthew 18:15-19

❓ *What are the step-by-step instructions to addressing sin in others?*

❓ *Why do you think this approach is wise or necessary?*

❓ *What part of God's character lies behind this approach?*

This attitude to sin flows from a deep appreciation of the love of God. We are called to...

- **forgive like God.** As Christians we've been forgiven by God. Great gratitude should lead to a great desire to forgive in the same way.

- **love like God.** Remember, offences against us are no reason for not loving. God loved us when we were a total offence to him (see Romans 5:8-9).

- **overlook much.** We may want (even deserve) an apology. Scripture encourages us to overlook much. Check out Colossians 3:13; Proverbs 17:9; 19:11.

  ❓ *Which of these three do you find most difficult in practice?*

🔼 Pray

If people's offences against you loom larger in your mind than your sins against God, you'll never forgive. Pray that you'll see how much you've been forgiven.

Work at reconciliation

Re-read Luke 6:37; Matthew 18:15-19

❓ *Whose responsibility is it to initiate the process?*

❓ *What end points are possible or likely if we follow this pattern of loving forgiveness and reconciliation?*

❓ *What experience do you have of this in practice?*

Some more powerful points to consider.

- **Make overtures that may be rejected.** Even when you are sinned against, it's up to us to make overtures for peace. It's what God did!

- **Want the best for them** (Matthew 18:15). Don't demand an apology for offended pride; aim to win back a brother.

- **Get the church involved.** God has given his church a role in judging (see 1 Corinthians 6:1-6). Done well this will avoid hidden resentments festering for years.

- **When someone doesn't want forgiveness it can't be given** (Matthew 18:17) . Similarly, God's gracious forgiveness of us is unconditional, but it's up to us to accept it. Stay ready to forgive, but don't blame yourself if it is not accepted.

- **Where someone wants forgiveness there will never be a time when we can say "No"** (Matthew 18:21-22). Seventy-seven times isn't a limit, but an endless number of times.

The God who thunders

In this psalm, God's voice is likened to the roaring thunder of a violent storm as it sweeps in from the sea.

Read Psalm 29

What are we to do?
Read Psalm 29:1-2

❷ *What, exactly, are we being called to do when David calls us to "ascribe to the LORD glory and strength"? The words may be familiar, but what exactly does it mean in practice?*

Ascribe seems such a weak word—as if we are to make sure that "glory" and "strength" are on the list of things that you think God is like. But, actually, it's much more than that.

❷ *Why do you think that he calls on the "Mighty Ones" (v 1, ESV) to do this?*

David may be referring to angelic beings, or to the great people of his land: the leaders, mighty warriors, etc. Whoever he is referring to, the continuing problem for able people is that we assume that our achievements are down to us (wrong); that our skills belong to us (they don't); and that we deserve recognition from others for what we do (wrong again!). Anything great, or beautiful or successful in your life—your work, your marriage, your church, your family—is actually God's achievement, not yours.

⌄ Apply

Maybe you need to spend time now before

God repenting of your proud attitude. Everything that you have comes from him. Everything of value that you achieve is really his doing. And all the respect and appreciation that others have shown to you really belongs to him. Hand it all over to the rightful owner now. *Ascribe...*

Why are we to do it?
Read Psalm 29:3-11

❷ *Why, do you think, is the image of a storm for God particularly appropriate?*

Uncontrollable. Unstoppable. Totally outside our ability to manipulate. All we can do is batten down the hatches and cower in our storm shelter until it blows over. It does exactly as it wishes, and we cannot influence it in any way at all.

❷ *What reason does David give for our need for humility in verse 11?*

Our God doesn't exercise his awesome power just to please himself. His desire is to pour out blessings of peace on his own people. But woe betide those who have received those blessings if they forget where it all comes from...

⌃ Pray

Praise the Lord for all that he does for you as shown in verse 11.

Bible in a year: 2 Kings 19 – 21 • Matthew 15:21-39

The importance of others

Love God and love your neighbour are the two greatest commands, according to Jesus. But what is the relationship between the two?

Really loving God

Read Luke 6:27-38

❓ *How many of these verses are about how we should love God?*

❓ *How many are about how we should love others?*

This was of course a trick question. The answer is they are all about both. Because loving God is inseparable from loving others.

Read Luke 10:25-37

❓ *What is the order of priority here?*

❓ *What is the link between them?*

❓ *What is the big idea in this parable?*

There is a priority here. Loving the Lord comes before loving others. But there is also an inseparable link. We are not really loving God if we are not really loving others. That is one of the main points of the parable. The priest and Levite were very religious. They "loved God" very much. Except they didn't— because they didn't love their neighbour. In that, they were put to shame by the lowly, despised Samaritan.

❓ *Do we tend to think that God calls us to love him, and that drives us to love others?*

❓ *Is it possible to love God without loving others?*

Jesus says it is not. It is as if he puts others between us and himself and says, "You love me through them".

So not this:

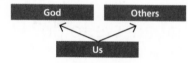

But this:

⌄ Apply

It's very easy to do what the priest and Levite did. They were both strong on religious activity but not on relationships. But holiness is about relationships (with God and others). There are all sorts of religious things that are good to do—Bible reading and prayer, for example. But they are not an end in themselves. They are a means to an end. Holiness is not simply lots of Bible reading and prayer. It's also learning to love God by loving others.

❓ *How about a reality check. What are you known for among your colleagues, friends and family? Being religious? Or being a good Samaritan?*

Self-centred?

Why is it that I get what I give? Isn't that just a self-centred motive for being godly?
"You are only a Christian because you want heaven—and that's just self-centred".

❓ *How do you react to the accusation above? Do you think it is valid?*

Inconsistent?

Read Luke 6:37-38

❓ *What hints might there be in Jesus' teaching that this is not a problem?*

It is striking that after all his prohibitions on a tit-for-tat attitude (v 27-36), Jesus does seem to be suggesting that we should bear in mind the payback for godliness. It really *does* deliver results.

···· **TIME OUT** ····································

Consider how often God tells us that he longs to be a blessing to us. If you need any encouragement on this then check out Isaiah 35:1-10 and Matthew 11:28-30. Praise the Lord that he is what we do not deserve—the God of wonderful blessing!

What's the explanation?

❓ *What do you think the honest reply to the accusation of self-centredness should be?*

We touched on this when we looked at what Jesus meant by reward (Luke 6:35). The reward is God himself—and in the Bible it is never wrong to want God for myself. To look for blessing in God is not self-centred but God-centred, not sinful but obedient. To

object to salvation because it does us good is not selfless—it's masochism!

It's true that we can be self-centred about God—if we keep him to ourselves. This is another implication of the parable of the good Samaritan (Luke 10:25-37), that we were looking at yesterday.

Jesus is saying that if we *really* love God (unlike the priest and the Levite, but like the Samaritan), we will become *like* God. It's as if the mercy and loving kindness of God infects our lives with a sort of holy disease. If we have really seen what God is like and drunk of his mercy, we will be infected with mercy—and infectious with mercy. We will always be spreading it with our attitudes, our actions and our words.

And if we are not infected with mercy, or infectious, then clearly, we have not drunk of it at all.

⌄ Apply

❓ *How could you spread the holy infection of mercy today in a world that is naturally free of it?*

⌃ Pray

Pray through the day ahead.

Overflowing God

We've been spending a lot of time on these two verses, because the ideas in them recur in Jesus' teaching again and again. Let's think about them one more time.

Mercy leads to mercy

Read Luke 6:37-38

❓ *What imagery is being used in verse 38? What is the imaginative picture it creates in our minds?*

❓ *So what is the Lord trying to convey to us about our attitude towards other people, and towards love, mercy and forgiveness?*

A merchant would shake corn down in his measuring cup so that the customer got a full measure. That was then poured into a pocket made from a fold in the customer's garment (translated "lap").

The Jewish rabbis used to say that God measured using one of two weighing scales—justice or mercy. By contrast, the Lord Jesus says, "With the measure you use, it will be measured to you". In other words, the way we behave towards others shows how we think people should be treated by God. Some are very keen to see others judged because they think that they themselves will receive a positive judgment. Of course, they are completely wrong (v 37). Other people show mercy to others. They know that unless mercy is the order of the day, they have no hope of acceptance before the throne of God.

And mercy overflows

❓ *What happens if we use the mercy "measure" for everyone (v 38)?*

❓ *What exactly are the merciful blessings of God towards us beyond forgiveness for our sins?*

God's measure of mercy to us is not just full—it is overflowing. His mercy to me massively outweighs any mercy I ever show. And what are the merciful blessings of God? Here are just a few.

- Forgiveness (v 37). The context here is the blessing of living a forgiven life, not just escaping condemnation.

- The blessings of living in relationship with God and the blessings of eternal life (see Luke 18:29-30).

- Answered prayer (John 15:7).

- Inexpressible joy (1 Peter 1:8-9).

❓ *What would you add to the list?*

☑ Apply

Why is it that so many of us have so little joy in Christ, that we seem to know so little answered prayer, etc? Maybe it is because we're not much into showing mercy ourselves.

Make me a channel of your peace...
It is in pardoning that we are pardoned,
in giving to all men that we receive...

Good teaching matters

The marks of mercy are not just things we should seek in our own lives, but are crucial elements in the lives of those who teach and lead us.

At this point in his sermon, Jesus seems to move on to a third section of teaching.

- **Section 1** (v 20-26): Christian counter-culture
- **Section 2** (v 27-38): Mercy-minded.
- **Section 3** (v 39-49): Words matter.

Words matter
Read Luke 6:39-40

❓ *What is the main point of these verses?*
❓ *How does this follow on from the previous passage?*

The main point is that it matters who teaches us about God. In fact, it matters very much, because if we follow a "blind guide", we could fall into a pit (v 39). So...

✔ Apply

- **Beware ungodly teachers.** "The student is not above the teacher." The lives of those who teach us really matter. Paul agreed. His lists of qualifications for being a teacher in the church are all about godliness of life (1 Timothy 3:1-7; Titus 1:5-9).

- **Beware judgmental teachers.** Given what's gone before, the most obvious "blindness" is that which thinks we can judge and don't need forgiveness.

  ❓ *Do we ask ourselves how "mercy minded" our teachers are? Jesus thinks it is vital.*

- **Beware our own sin.** Many of us sooner or later end up with some teaching role—Sunday school, youth work, homegroup, or our own children. Don't forget what James said, "Not many of you should become teachers, my fellow believers, because you know that we who teach will be judged more strictly." (James 3:1). "What my congregation needs most is my personal holiness", said one great preacher—how true!

- **Follow Jesus.** Many voices call for our attention today. Whose words do we listen to? They are all blind guides except one. Only one can really teach us the ways of mercy. The role of the Christian teacher is to speak Jesus' words, and encourage people to follow Christ's ways.

  ❓ *Is that what your teachers do—or is their focus something other than Jesus?*
  ❓ *If you are a teacher, are you passionate about sharing Jesus, or is your focus somewhere else?*

▲ Pray

There is a vital need to make sure we are listening to the right teachers—but also a vital need to pray for our teachers, and for ourselves as teachers.

❓ *Why not pray through each of today's points for your own leaders and for yourself?*

Words for others

Jesus started this section by talking about words from teachers. Now he goes on to talk about words of criticism which anyone may use.

Sawdust

Read Luke 6:41-42

❷ *Look at the two people described in these verses—how are they similar and how are they different?*

❷ *What is Jesus' main concern?*

Just imagine it. Here comes Jill with a large plank in her eye—and she is trying to see to take a bit of sawdust out of Sarah's eye. *Ridiculous!* And hypocritical! And useless! It is Jill who needs the help of course—much more than Sarah.

Now imagine what Jesus is really talking about. Beth has a massive temper problem. She is always cross when people get in her way or don't do what she wants. Then she starts trying to help Sarah, who has lost her cool once or twice recently when she was overtired. *Ridiculous!* And hypocritical! And useless! Sarah isn't likely to learn much from someone who is so "way off" herself.

Or maybe the context of verse 37 is still in Jesus' mind. After all, it is certainly very difficult to learn from someone who is judgmental. Rob happens to find it quite easy to control his temper and so looks down on Sarah for her failings. He starts lecturing Sarah about her anger problem, or perhaps gets at her about her quiet times or prayer-meeting attendance, or any number of things—failing to see the massive plank of self-righteousness in his own eye.

Here's a final scenario. Oscar sees that Sarah has a bit of a problem with her temper. But he's aware that he is judgmental, or he knows he has some hopeless and obvious area of failure himself. He's upset—because he knows that, as he is, he cannot help Sarah. So, he goes away and prays and plans and gets rid of his "plank", so that there might just be the chance to help his sister Sarah.

⌄ Apply

❷ *Are you Beth, Rob or Oscar?*

❷ *Where are your "planks" likely to be? Why not get them out ahead of time— for Jesus' sake, your sake and the sake of others?*

And plead with the Lord to deal with you. Because you can't do it without his rebuke, enlightenment, grace, forgiveness and the Spirit's life-changing power.

Getting the heart right

Planks are obvious. But religious hypocrisy is much harder to spot. So what are the subtle signs that someone is a false teacher or a fake disciple?

Good fruit, bad fruit

Read Luke 6:43-45

❷ What makes for good fruit (v 43)?
❷ How do you tell a good tree (v 44)?
❷ How many kinds of "trees" are there (v 43, 45)?
❷ What is the simple but profound message here?

To grow good fruit you need to be a good tree. Look at v 43. Good tree—good fruit; bad tree—bad fruit. In order to produce what Jesus thinks is good fruit, then we must be—or become—good trees. And there are only good trees and bad trees.

Re-read Luke 6:43-45

There seem to be many sorts of people in the world—but Jesus actually recognises only two sorts. It is God who makes us good trees. Elsewhere, Jesus makes it clear that we are all "bad" by nature (look up Mark 7:1-2, 14-23). We only truly become "good" when God's grace changes our lives.

⌄ Apply

The tree analogy helps us hold together two facts. First, that we are saved by God's grace and not by good works; and second that good works are a necessary part of being saved. A good tree will always produce good fruit. Is there no good fruit? Then it is not a good tree. God's grace always leads to good

works (see Ephesians 2:10). Are there no good works? Then there has been no real work of grace.

❷ But how easy is it for us to detect these differences in ourselves and others?

Warnings

Re-read Luke 6:43-45

❷ What attitudes do you think we need to have to make wise and careful judgments in this area?

We do not see others as God sees them, and so we need real humility. We have no window into the souls of others, and so we may misinterpret the evidence. We should be very slow to pass judgment on other people's salvation. Jesus' words are meant to challenge our own lives.

And we need to realise that sanctification is a gradual process. Jesus' analogies often make just one point—the picture is filled out elsewhere in Scripture, showing that after we are saved, sin remains within us. Producing fruit from God is something that comes gradually, as we co-operate with God's work in our lives by the Spirit (see Galatians 5:25).

⌃ Pray

Pray for a heart that loves what he loves and a life that shows the same.

Salvation song

This is a song of thanksgiving that David wrote, possibly after an illness.

I've been saved

Read Psalm 30:1-3

❓ *List the particular reasons why David is so thankful.*

🔼 Pray

I'm saved, praise the Lord! But it's good to dwell in detail on all the aspects of that. Spend some time thanking God now for...

- how he led you to be saved and the people he used.
- what he saved you from: hell and the devil's influence, certainly, but also from futility and false directions in life.
- how he has answered your prayers over the years.
- his sheer grace in saving you, when you didn't (and still don't) deserve it.
- how he is healing the marks and stains of sin in your life.

By whom

Read Psalm 30:4-5

Luther called God's anger "God's strange work" because wrath is not a part of God's character in the same way that love is. God's wrath is called into being by our sinfulness and rebellion—it is temporal and temporary. But there has always been and always will be love throughout eternity because of the relationship of love between the Father and the Son in the Trinity. That is why "his anger lasts only a moment, but his favour lasts a lifetime" (v 5).

🔽 Apply

How, basically, do you think about the Lord: as an angry God who also loves us? Or as a loving God who is angry at our sin? Although the difference may appear subtle, the latter is the truly liberating truth.

For what

Read Psalm 30:6-12

❓ *So what is the fundamental reason that we have been saved, according to these verses?*

Praising God features big in David's understanding of the reason why he has been saved. And not only praising God himself, but also declaring his praise to others (v 9).

🔼 Pray

It is actually the reason that you are alive today: to serve God, to praise him, and to declare his greatness to others. So...

- praise him now that he has rescued you.
- ask him to show you ways you can better serve him.
- cry to him for opportunities to speak to others about Christ today.

 Bible in a year: Jeremiah 1 – 2 • Matthew 20:17-34

Our words matter

Apparently, we speak, on average, 7,000 words a day. That's a lot of talking. But Jesus is concerned about the quality of our words, not the quantity.

Words that reveal

Read Luke 6:43-46

> ❷ *What one sort of "fruit" particularly reveals the kind of tree we are?*
> ❷ *What sort of words conceal what we really are?*
> ❷ *How might this be different to what the world believes?*

This third section of Jesus' sermon (from verse 39 onwards) has been about words. Jesus thinks our words matter because they particularly reveal what we are really like. "For the mouth speaks what the heart is full of" (v 45).

Most people believe that harmful words result from the force of external pressures disrupting our normally pleasant, polite natures. We tend to blame our circumstances: "I was tired / ill / stressed out. I wasn't myself when I said that". We speak of "slips of the tongue" and saying something in an "off-moment".

But Jesus actually pre-empts modern psychology. According to him, the slips are what we might call "Freudian slips". In other words, they reveal what is really there—deep down. According to Jesus, as with all evil behaviour, the source of evil speech is sinful hearts (Mark 7:20)—our words are a very good index of our spiritual state.

Words that conceal

Re-read Luke 6:43-46

> ❷ *What's the exception to this rule (v 46)?*

Words are a good index of our spiritual state—with one big exception. It is possible to be a hypocrite and to pretend to be something we are not. To call Jesus "Lord" but not to obey him is to conceal what we really are. Sometimes actions speak louder than words. More on this tomorrow.

☑ Apply

> ❷ *How does evil speech show up in your life? Is it being untruthful, demeaning of others, angry and abusive, gossipy, rash and insensitive, or hypocritical?*

Compare the words you use in church with those you speak in the privacy of your home—or your car, when you express your feelings towards other drivers.

> ❷ *What does that reveal about you? What do you need to do about it?*

☒ Pray

Pray against hypocrisy and for integrity. Hypocrisy uses words as a mask to cover up what we really are inside. We need an "integration" of our heart with our words and deeds so that they are all the same—the heart for Jesus producing words and works for him.

His words matter!

As Jesus draws his sermon to a close, he ends with a powerful illustration that gives each of us a stark warning…

Wise and foolish

Read Luke 6:46-49

❓ *Imagine a 21st-century version of the wise and foolish people in Jesus' story. Would they look different to us?*

❓ *When would the difference show?*

John has a daily quiet time (using a very good set of Bible-study notes). He reads Christian books and is in church every week, taking notes in sermons. Joe is identical—the same quiet-time routine, reading habits and conscientious attitude in church. There is just one difference. John lives it; Joe doesn't.

Joe isn't an obvious sinner—he's actually quite a nice guy. But, there are one or two significant areas—perhaps issues of money, relationships, sex or pride—where he makes no attempt to live for Christ at all. Consequently, his use of the word "Lord" rings hollow (v 46). The saying "If he is not Lord of all—he is not Lord at all" is true.

John, of course, has his faults—big ones, and in some ways they are more obvious than Joe's. But step by painful step, in every area, he is seeking to bring himself under the command of Christ. Most of us would think their two "houses" are just the same. But the storm of judgment will show they could not be more different.

Back at the beginning of this sermon, we saw that Jesus was giving us his law for our

good and blessing. What greater blessing could there be than that our lives stand firm at God's judgment?

⌄ Apply

The ancient Greeks tended to divide body, soul and spirit. They thought that understanding was something that happened in the mind. The Hebrews knew that something had not been "understood" unless it showed in life. Jesus says that it is our lives that will show we have understood him.

So, when we come to the Bible, what are we satisfied with? A feeling of encouragement, a challenge, an interesting point to store away for the next Bible study, a truth to chew over? These may be steps along the way to "understanding". But, if they are the end point, we have not really understood Jesus at all. Nothing short of an obedient life satisfies him.

⌃ Pray

It's time to take on board the challenge of verse 47. Review the whole sermon and write down three specific changes you need to make in response to God's word. Think, plan, then pray—but don't neglect to put into practice.

1

2

3

NEHEMIAH: Rebuilt to build

Nehemiah is nestled at the beginning of what's called the Second Temple Period (around 516 BC – 70 AD). God's people had been in captivity, but now they were returning to their own land.

Read Nehemiah 1:1-4

Among those who have already returned to Jerusalem is Hanani, the brother of Nehemiah. He comes to see Nehemiah in Susa, the capital of Persia (the empire that ruled over God's people at the time).

❷ *What does Hanani say about the people in Jerusalem?*
❷ *What does he say about the city itself?*
❷ *How does Nehemiah respond? Why do you think he feels this way?*

It's no wonder people feel broken. Without city walls to defend them and to keep the city inside intact, they are wrecked and without help.

But it isn't just about the physical destruction. Jerusalem was always about something bigger than just being a beautiful city or a well-defended one. It was the dwelling place of God. It was supposed to be the place where God's people represented him to the nations.

A city and a light

Read Exodus 19:5-6

These are words spoken by God to Moses.

❷ *What was involved in being God's people?*

This applies to us as followers of Jesus because we are now God's people—the ones who represent him to the world. Jesus said we are "the light of the world" and "a town built on a hill" which "cannot be hidden" (Matthew 5:14). In fact, Revelation describes the future of the church as being a "new Jerusalem"—a perfect city in which God dwells.

God wants us to be like movie trailers for that city—the perfect community. He sends us as his representatives into the world.

So what we are thinking through in Nehemiah is this: what is it like to see the power of the gospel transform and rebuild us into a reflection of the eternal Jerusalem?

⌄ Apply

Think about your church, your community, your country and your world.

❷ *Where do you see brokenness and despair?*
❷ *What work do you know of that is already going on to bring gospel transformation? What further work needs to be done?*

You could make a list of individuals, groups and issues that you want to pray for. You can refer back to this as you read Nehemiah.

First things first

Nehemiah cares so much about God's kingdom that he feels broken when he doesn't see God's rule represented as it should be.

At the start of chapter 2, he'll take action. But first, he prays.

Read Nehemiah 1:4-11

❓ *How does Nehemiah start his prayer (v 5)?*
❓ *How do you think that helps him?*

Nehemiah is setting his prayer up. He is naming the attributes of God that he is going to need. He starts by saying, *God, you know who you are. You know you are powerful and loyal.* Then he will ask God to act based on those characteristics.

❓ *Think about the issues and people you're praying about at the moment. What characteristics of God do you need to remember? How can you ask God to act based on those characteristics?*

Confessing sin

Besides acknowledging who God is, we also have to acknowledge who we are.

❓ *What sins does Nehemiah confess (v 6-7)?*

He's praying on behalf of his whole nation and so he asks for forgiveness for generations of sin. He doesn't blame anybody else. He confesses this sin as if he's a participant.

❓ *How could you pray this way for your community?*

Praying God's word

❓ *What does Nehemiah ask God to remember (v 8-9)?*
❓ *Why is this promise relevant to Nehemiah's situation?*
❓ *What promises to God's people today could you make use of to help you pray for your own situation?*

Asking in faith

Only at this point does Nehemiah make his request to the Lord.

❓ *What's his specific request (v 11)?*

Nehemiah is the king's servant, and he's going to leverage that position for the sake of his people and God's glory. He knows that the king is powerful; but God is the one who is truly sovereign over Nehemiah's circumstances.

❓ *What specific help do you need from God?*
❓ *How can you express faith and trust in his command over your circumstances?*

Nehemiah started this prayer mourning. But now he is ready to go before the king.

◢ Pray

Use the questions above to help you pray for yourself, your church and the wider community.

Going before the king

Where do you live? What do you do? Do you ever think about how God has placed you there for a purpose?

Nehemiah is the cupbearer to King Artaxerxes (Nehemiah 1:11). In chapter 2, he leverages that position for God's purposes.

Read Nehemiah 2:1-8

This is a festive time. Everyone is enjoying themselves—except Nehemiah. At this point Nehemiah has been praying and fasting for four months. He has been coming before God with a broken heart.

❷ *What does Artaxerxes notice about Nehemiah (v 2)?*

In Nehemiah's day, you didn't come before the king sad. You'd run the risk of getting your head chopped off! So Nehemiah is shaken (v 2). Yet he chooses to risk his life and use the opportunity he has.

A wise interaction

❷ *How does Nehemiah show respect towards the king (v 3)?*
❷ *How does he explain his sadness?*

Nehemiah contextualizes the information for Artaxerxes. The king wouldn't understand that Jerusalem was God's city, but he could imagine that you would care about your ancestral city. This is a lesson in how to wisely engage with unbelievers: find common ground. The result is that the king is ready to listen.

❷ *What does Nehemiah do next (v 4)?*
❷ *What request does he make (v 5)?*

In the following verses we see that Nehemiah has already made meticulous plans. He knows exactly what he needs from the king.

❷ *What does he ask for (v 6-8)?*
❷ *What is he planning to do?*

The letters are for protection. They would show he was on official business and stop people attacking him.

Success

❷ *Why does Nehemiah get what he asks for (v 8)?*

Nehemiah was respectful and persuasive. He had planned meticulously and been diligent in prayer. Yet none of this would have been any use if God hadn't been behind him. The surest way to experience God's helping hands is to seek his heart first: to spend time with him, repent of sin, live obediently and seek his will.

⌄ Apply

This passage teaches us how to use an ordinary conversation for God's glory: finding common ground, praying before and during conversations, planning what to say or suggest and seeking God's will above all else.

❷ *Where has God placed you? What regular interactions do you have?*
❷ *How could you be like Nehemiah in those interactions?*

Bible in a year: Jeremiah 15 – 17 • Matthew 23:1-22

Let us build

What does it look like when we are concerned for the things God is concerned for?

First off, it always ruffles things up among God's opponents.

Read Nehemiah 2:9-16

❓ *Why do Sanballat and Tobiah oppose Nehemiah (v 10)?*

Vision and planning

❓ *What does Nehemiah do when he arrives in Jerusalem (v 12-15)?*
❓ *Who does he tell about his plans (v 12, 16)?*

It's interesting to note Nehemiah's confidence about his vision for rebuilding Jerusalem. He calls it "what my God had put in my heart to do" (v 12). He knows it is God working through him.

At the same time, he needs to test his plans carefully before he makes them known.

It's important not to confuse vision with plans. God may give you a vision for something—you are confident that it comes from him and is in line with his word. You should pursue that vision wholeheartedly. But many times the specific plans you make to get there will need to change.

Working together

Nehemiah is now ready to call the people in Jerusalem together and share his vision.

Read Nehemiah 2:17-20

Notice that he doesn't say, *Look at this mess. My goodness. You should be ashamed of yourselves.* No, he says, "You see the trouble we are in". He includes himself as one of the people.

The ownership of the solution is also mutual. Nehemiah doesn't say, *Let me build the walls for you.* He says, "Let us rebuild". In order to establish unity among them, he also tells them of what God has been doing (v 18)—recognizing that God is the initiator of everything.

This is a call on God's people today, too. We are called to build God's kingdom together.

❓ *How have you seen "the hand of [your] God" at work recently?*
❓ *Who could you tell about this—to encourage them, too, to build for God?*

The God of heaven

❓ *How do Nehemiah's enemies respond to the news that the people are ready to start the work (v 19)?*
❓ *What does Nehemiah say next (v 20)?*

⌃ Pray

Praise God that he is "the God of heaven"—sovereign over everything. Ask for his help in building his kingdom in your community. Pray that he would give you vision, and ask for his help in planning the practical steps to make that vision happen.

Bible in a year: Jeremiah 18 – 19 • Matthew 23:23-39

In a tight spot

David's in a tight spot. His enemies are looming large, and his friends have left him in the lurch. No prizes for guessing where he turns in his hour of crisis...

Firm in the fortress

Read Psalm 31:1-4

❓ *What specifically does David want God to do for him?*

❓ *What powerful image does he have of God?*

❓ *Why should God help him?*

David's enemies have laid a trap for him (v 4), but he seeks refuge, deliverance and safety in a fortress—the Lord (v 3). He knows he can stand firmly and safely in this fortress. All around him is fear and anguish, but he has the antidote to this crisis— prayerful refuge in a mighty fortress—the Lord. And notice that it is for "the sake of [God's] name". David's ultimate desire is to see God honoured (v 3b).

Commitment

Read Psalm 31:5

❓ *What leaves you feeling surrounded, trapped, left in the lurch?*

❓ *How do you react? In a flailing panic?*

❓ *What is David's response to a desperate situation?*

David doesn't lash out at everything in sight. And he doesn't roll up into a tiny ball of self-pity. He commits this situation—in fact his whole life (spirit)—into God's hands. He shows his loyalty and his trust in the Lord.

TIME OUT

Does verse 5 ring any bells with you? Look up **Luke 23:44-46**.

Then read **Acts 7:59-60** and **1 Peter 4:19**. The Lord Jesus is the ultimate example of committing his life to God. Literally.

Who do you trust?

Read Psalm 31:6-8

❓ *Why do you think he "hates" the people in verse 6?*

❓ *What is the difference between them and him?*

❓ *What is the difference between idols and the Lord?*

Our trust should solely be in the Lord. Not in ourselves, not in others, not in superstitions and worthless idols (v 6). Our confidence is in God, for he knows our troubles and sees our anguish (v 7). Only he can lead us to safety (v 8).

◢ Pray

Feeling harassed? Trapped? Alone? Then follow David's example—you know where to turn. Will you commit your life into God's hands and trust in his promise of eternal refuge?

Jesus is the mighty fortress that we can be safe in. All other options are worthless.

Human hands

What does it look like for the gracious hand of God (Nehemiah 2:18) to be at work?

In this case, it looks like him appointing his people to be a part of his rebuilding initiative.

Read Nehemiah 3:1-32 (or if you have less time, just verses 1-9)

Building together

It is significant that the high priest is the first person mentioned among those helping to rebuild the wall. Nehemiah doesn't mention the merchants yet, or the politicians, or the regular labourers. He begins with the spiritual leaders, who set the tone for how the work was to be done. When a leader serves, it motivates the rest of the people to serve, too.

❓ *What other types of people do we see building the wall (v 8, 9, 12, 32)?*

People from all walks of life were working together. This was a broken-down city, but they knew God had called them there.

✔ Apply

❓ *Are you ever tempted to think you can't be part of God's mission today? Why?*
❓ *How does this passage help and encourage you?*
❓ *How could you get involved in God's work?*
❓ *Who else could you encourage to join in?*

What is built is God's

❓ *What's the first thing that is built (v 1)?*

Consecrate (or dedicate) means "set something aside for a unique task". In Hebrew it is related to the word "holy". They are pointing, first, to the fact that this entire project is set aside as a unique task for God's sake and, second, to the fact that it belongs to God.

To consecrate the gate, the priests would have smeared either oil or blood on it. Whenever anyone saw the blood or smelled the oil, they would be reminded that this gate was special and that it was God's.

The Sheep Gate was important because it was where sacrificial animals were brought into the city. These sacrifices pointed to Jesus' sacrifice on the cross, which finally secured salvation for sinners. So it shouldn't surprise us that the Sheep Gate is built first and specially consecrated. It's ultimately a symbol of the cross—which is what we should place as central in our own ministry.

✔ Apply

❓ *Is proclaiming the cross the centre and priority of your church and your life?*
❓ *Your ministry might involve many practical and social issues. But how can you ensure that the gospel sets the tone?*

Angry opponents

Whenever we sense God's presence and experience his provision, we have to take into account the fact that there is someone out there who doesn't like that at all.

Every time we move forward in what God has called us to do, there is going to be opposition.

So how do we deal with it?

Read Nehemiah 4:1-9

❓ *How do Sanballat and Tobiah try to discourage the builders (v 1-3)?*

TIME OUT

Sanballat doesn't understand how God works. God *does* like to use broken and burnt stones that have been rejected. This is most obviously true of Jesus—the stone that the builders rejected, which became the chief cornerstone (Matthew 21:42; Psalm 118:22). But in a different way, this is also true of us. God is near to the broken-hearted and close to those who are crushed in spirit (Psalm 34:18). He wants to use even the brokenness itself and the marks of the burning to honour his name. These things will show that it was God who revived and restored the person that was broken.

Vent in prayer

Nehemiah goes straight into a prayer (Nehemiah 4:4-5). He doesn't hold back from being honest with God about his hurt!

❓ *What does he ask God to do?*

When we're opposed, we need to let God handle it. Be angry, be hurt—but bring those things to God rather than lashing out.

Nehemiah isn't passive: we'll see him take Sanballat and Tobiah seriously. But before he acts, he cries out to God.

Stay focused

❓ *What do the people do next (v 6)?*

Nehemiah doesn't let opposition change his vision. He trusts God.

Unsurprisingly, though, the opposition intensifies.

❓ *What further opposition do God's people encounter (v 7-8)?*

Sanballat's group, the Samaritans, are from the north; the Arabs are from the south, the Ashdodites are from the west, and the Ammonites are from the east. Between them they surround Jerusalem.

But God's people aren't fazed (v 9). They take sensible precautions to make sure they can keep going. And they focus on God, their help and their strength. He is the one who has allowed the opposition to intensify. He is bigger than their circumstances. They can trust him.

⌃ Pray

What difficulties are you facing right now? Or who do you know who is facing opposition in their ministry? Pray for those situations in the light of what you have read.

Finding strength

Discouragement upon discouragement means that strength has begun to fail among the wall-builders in Jerusalem.

Read Nehemiah 4:10-14

❷ *What kind of strength is needed, do you think (v 10)?*

❷ *What two sources of discouragement are there (v 11-12)?*

When we meet with opposition, we have to decide: is it worth it to continue?

❷ *What does Nehemiah think (v 13-14)?*

❷ *How does he help the builders to feel stronger?*

Fight for God's glory

Fighting is part of being a Christian. As we build, we have to learn how to fight. There is nothing worthwhile that God has called us to build that we won't have to fight for while we build it.

But we don't fight alone. Nehemiah doesn't simply tell the people to muster up their energy in the flesh. He tells them to look at who God is (v 14). Only after they have remembered what God is really like does he tell them to fight.

❷ *How does Nehemiah describe God?*

❷ *How do you think the people might have felt as they heard this description?*

Fight for God's people

In the New Testament, terms related to physical fighting are used to describe the spiritual battle we face. When Paul says, "I have fought the good fight," he means he has "kept the faith"—he has persevered (2 Timothy 4:7). Nehemiah's literal call to fight may at first seem far removed from this type of spiritual fighting. But bear in mind that Paul's spiritual fight was not just about maintaining his own beliefs. He fought for other people. He endured hardship upon hardship in order to bring the gospel to communities across the Mediterranean and to encourage and build up his fellow believers.

❷ *Who does Nehemiah call the people to fight for (Nehemiah 4:14)?*

The word "brothers" (ESV) doesn't just mean "family members." It means people from the same country or ethnicity as you. In a New Testament context the word "brothers" means all Christians—including sisters, of course!

⌄ Apply

❷ *Think about the Christian brothers and sisters around you. What would it look like to fight for them this week?*

❷ *What about your biological family members? How could you fight for God's glory in their lives?*

Whether we feel weak or strong, we need to remember to find our purpose in God. "Remember the Lord"—then fight for whatever is an opportunity to give him glory.

Work worth defending

The inhabitants of Jerusalem have stopped their work to defend the walls. Enemies surround them. The situation doesn't look good.

Yet after Nehemiah's call to "remember the Lord" and fight (4:14), the tide turns.

Read Nehemiah 4:15-23

> ❷ *What has frustrated the enemies' plans (look back at v 13)?*
> ❷ *Who is responsible for this (v 15)?*

Build and defend

But Nehemiah knows that God's enemies have not gone away. The rest of this chapter shows how he combines defence and development—building the wall, yet always being ready to stop and fight.

> ❷ *What steps are taken to enable both building and defence (v 16-19)?*
> ❷ *What other precautions does Nehemiah take (v 19-20, 21-23)?*
> ❷ *Who is ultimately responsible for defending the work (v 20)?*

▾ Apply

Jude verse 3 sheds light on the balance between building and defending in the church today. "Dear friends, although I was very eager to write to you about the salvation we share, I felt compelled to write and urge you to contend for the faith that was once for all entrusted to God's holy people." Jude could have written to "build"—to help his readers understand more about their salvation. But instead he focused on "defence": urging

them to stick to what they already knew.

> ❷ *What could you do to "build" in your church?*
> ❷ *Where is "defence" necessary?*

One work

In Nehemiah 4:15, they all return to the wall, "each to *our own* work". But in verse 17, it's called "*the* work" (ESV). They have different tasks, but they're united around one work.

Today, too, there is only one work of God on our planet: the work of the worldwide church in reaching lost people. We may have a church here and a person there, but it all belongs to God. We are simply rallying around him and joining him.

But within the big work of God, everybody has an assignment. Each person is a small part of the grand scheme.

▾ Apply

> ❷ *In what ways are you part of God's work in your local community?*
> ❷ *Do you ever fall into the trap of taking too much ownership over that work?*
> ❷ *Do you ever fall into the trap of thinking the work you do is not really good enough to be part of God's work?*
> ❷ *How does what you've just read encourage or challenge you?*

A great outcry

What injustices do you see in the world around you—whether big or small? How do you think God feels about them?

In chapter 5 we turn to see problems within Jerusalem itself: a serious case of injustice.

Read Nehemiah 5:1-13

❷ *What's the initial cause of the problem (v 2, 3)?*
❷ *What are people forced to do (v 3)?*
❷ *What's the other source of economic difficulty (v 4)?*
❷ *How are people forced to respond (v 5)?*

Human resources were already squeezed because of the necessity of defending the city. There weren't enough men to staff the farms. That was why there was not enough food. And certain people were taking advantage of this situation to exploit their poorer brethren (v 7).

In this culture, when you couldn't pay your bills, you used your possessions and property as collateral. When those ran out, you had to put your children into temporary slavery until they had worked off your debt.

❷ *What hints do we get at how the people feel about this situation (v 1, 5)?*

The fear of God

❷ *What's Nehemiah's immediate reaction (v 6)?*
❷ *What action does he take (v 7)?*

Nehemiah has actually bought the freedom of some of the people from foreign masters (v 8). But now the nobles are selling into

slavery the very people they should welcome as their brothers.

Nehemiah says they should be walking in the fear of God (v 9). Injustice isn't simply what humans have decided is wrong; it is contrary to God's nature. If we know God, if we are awestruck by him, it should make us reach out to help others, not to exploit them.

Doing justice

❷ *What does Nehemiah tell the nobles they must do (v 10-11)?*

He guarantees justice and reparation for the oppressed. At the same time, instead of punishing the oppressors, he gives them a second chance. He calls them to repentance.

They have a second chance, but if they go back to their sinful ways, they will run out of chances (v 13). God's grace is abundant, but we do have to take our sin seriously and turn to him in genuine repentance.

◤ Pray

Are you guilty of having exploited a brother or sister in Christ in any way? Confess your sin and ask for God's help to repent and repair what you've done.

Reflecting on God's perfect justice, pray for unjust situations you see around you. Ask God to help you see how to bring justice.

Bible in a year: Jeremiah 32 – 33 • Matthew 26:26-50

Surrendering rights

In modern Western cultures we think a lot about our rights. We know what we're entitled to and we make sure we get it.

But in Nehemiah's example we see a different way of thinking about rights.

Read Nehemiah 5:14-19

❷ *As governor, what does Nehemiah have the right to do (v 14-15)?*

Nehemiah has an entourage of about 150 men (v 17). He has to feed all of them.

❷ *How much food is being prepared for Nehemiah and his servants and guests each day (v 18)?*
❷ *How much do you think that would cost today?*

The money to pay for all this normally came out of taxes. Most governors wouldn't just raise what they really needed; they'd tax people hard so that they themselves could eat luxuriously and employ a lot of servants.

We know Nehemiah seeks to "walk in the fear of our God" (v 9) and act justly. So we might expect him not to exact heavy taxes but only what he really needs. Yet he goes one step further: he doesn't demand the governor's food allowance at all (v 14, 18).

❷ *Why not (v 18)?*
❷ *If Nehemiah did demand taxes, what would happen to the wall-building?*

Nehemiah is laying down his rights for the sake of the people and the wall-building project. He is looking for ways to make sure the mission of God gets done, without that being at the expense of the people of God.

❷ *What else does Nehemiah do—and not do (v 16)?*

Slave of all

Nehemiah's servant leadership is beautiful because we see Jesus in it.

❷ *How did Jesus surrender his rights for the sake of his people?*

In Mark 10:42-44, Jesus said to his followers, "You know that those who are regarded as rulers of the Gentiles lord it over them, and their high officials exercise authority over them. Not so with you. Instead, whoever wants to become great among you must be your servant, and whoever wants to be first must be slave of all."

❷ *What would it look like for you to be "slave of all" this week—surrendering your rights and entitlements for the sake of others?*

⌃ Pray

❷ *What is Nehemiah's motivation (v 15)?*
❷ *How does his prayer in verse 19 show this?*

Nehemiah isn't so much asking for a reward as declaring that he has acted in good faith and from right motives.

Can you be that bold? Do you have a track record of acting according to his will? Pray in response to what you have read.

Bible in a year: Jeremiah 34 – 36 • Matthew 26:51-75 ⌄

From fear to faith

In the first part of Psalm 31, David turned to the Lord in a tight situation. He put his trust in God. Now David continues to pour his heart out...

Fear

Read Psalm 31:9-13

❷ *How does David feel?*

❷ *What does this tell us about the state of his heart and soul before God?*

David tells the Lord exactly how he feels. He is drained and distressed (v 9), weak and weary (v 10), forsaken (v 11), forgotten (v 12) and fearful (v 13). "Affliction" (v 10) can be translated as guilt or iniquity. David was not innocent, and he knew it. In some ways his own sin had been a contributory factor to his torment. But he knows that he can still turn to the Lord in trusting prayer.

···· TIME OUT ····································

Re-read verses 11-12: In the Bible, being abandoned (like a piece of broken pottery) by friends when times are tough seems quite common (see Psalm 38:11; Job 19:13-19; Jeremiah 12:6).

❷ *Why do you think people act that way?*
❷ *Are you guilty of it sometimes?*

Faith

Read Psalm 31:14-18

❷ *What is the only route that David sees out of his distressing situation?*

David knows that his only defence against his overwhelming enemies is dependence on God's faithfulness and judgment

through trust (v 15) and prayer (v 17). David knew that his "times are in your hands" (v 15), so he can confidently ask the Lord to deliver him from his enemies.

❷ *How do you feel about the prayer in verses 17-18?*

Acts of vengeful malice are out of order (Leviticus 19:18; Romans 12:19), but prayer for the downfall of ungodly persecutors (on a local or global scale) is biblical (1 Samuel 26:10-11; Psalm 5:10).

Thanks

Read Psalm 31:19-24

With hindsight, David looks back on his crisis and sees the Lord as being faithful as ever. The Lord shelters those who trust him (v 20) and answers those who cry out to him (v 22). No matter how alone and cut off from God we feel, we are never out of reach of his loving, protecting arms (v 22).

❷ *What should this knowledge spur us on to do (v 23-24)?*

⌄ Apply

❷ *How should these verses encourage you...*
- *when you doubt if you'll ever be able to keep going with God.*
- *when you doubt if he'll ever deal with those who oppose him.*
- *when you doubt he'll hear your prayers.*

Focus matters

You can have all the abilities and opportunities in the world, but if you don't have focus, you'll never get anything done.

That goes for our spiritual lives too. Focusing on Jesus is what enables us to be effective kingdom workers and bear fruit for him. Fortunately, God wants to teach us to focus. One way he does so is through adversity. In Nehemiah 6, the building of the wall is almost complete—and the enemy turns up the heat.

Read Nehemiah 6:1-14

❓ *How do Sanballat and Geshem try to stop the completion of the wall (v 2)?*
❓ *How does Nehemiah show his focus (v 3-4)?*

He knows and values what God has called him to do. That's how to stay focused— not only to know what God wants but also to value it when he shows it to us.

Character assassination

Finally, Sanballat tries something new. He sends an open letter (v 5)—one that anyone could read on the way to being delivered.

❓ *What does the letter accuse Nehemiah of (v 6-7)?*
❓ *How does Nehemiah respond (v 8-9)?*
❓ *What is he focusing on?*

Subtle distraction

Next, it's one of Nehemiah's own people who tries to take him off-focus. Shemaiah, one of the prophets (that is, someone who hears, or claims to hear, directly from God), tells Nehemiah that he is in danger and should take refuge in the temple (v 10). But Nehemiah says no: "I realised that God had not sent him" (v 12). Nobody but the priests was supposed to go into the temple. God would never tell Nehemiah to go in there.

❓ *Where does Shemaiah's "prophecy" really come from (v 12-13)?*
❓ *Why is it so important to Nehemiah not to go into the temple (v 11, 13)?*

No retaliation

Verse 14 is yet another example of Nehemiah's unflinching focus on God. Once again, he chooses not to retaliate or to try to deal with his enemies in his own strength. Once again, he offers up a prayer instead.

☑ Apply

Here are some ways we can remain on-focus as Christians:

- Know the Bible, which reveals God's will.
- Value what God values and seek his glory above anything else.
- Trust him when things go wrong, looking to him straight away for help, strength and guidance.

❓ *What could take you off-focus this week?*
❓ *What steps could you take to improve your focus on the Lord and his work?*

Rebuilding a people

The wall is finished—and in only 52 days!

Read Nehemiah 6:15 – 7:5

❷ *What do God's enemies think about this (6:16)?*

❷ *Why do you think that makes them think differently about themselves?*

Nevertheless, opposition to God's work doesn't end.

❷ *Who is fraternising with Tobiah and why (v 17-19)?*

❷ *What's Tobiah's aim (v 19)?*

❷ *Do you think he succeeded?*

This ongoing hostility is instructive for us. As believers, we are like a city protected by a wall. By dying on the cross, Jesus has put a protective barrier around us. His work of atonement is finished (John 19:30)! But for Nehemiah, completing the wall didn't put an end to all problems. It won't for us either. We still face trials, setbacks and opposition. Like Nehemiah, we should respond by putting our trust in the Lord.

Setting up the future

Nehemiah appoints key roles within the city. First are the gatekeepers who guard the wall and the singers and Levites who work in God's temple (7:1). Next he gives two men charge over the city.

❷ *Why does Nehemiah pick them (v 2)?*

❷ *How will they look after the city (v 3-4)?*

Now that the wall is rebuilt, the city itself can be developed and filled with people. Then it will really show off who the Lord is.

The remainder of the chapter is a list of all those who have returned from exile. Nehemiah plans to gather the people together and enrol them again (v 5).

Who's on the team?

Nehemiah wants to know who's actually part of God's people and who's ready to represent God's reign. We need this in our churches today: a deep level of community formation and commitment. We need to stand up to be counted.

Read Nehemiah 7:61-65

❷ *What's the problem in verses 61 and 64?*

These people aren't excluded from being part of Jerusalem—just from serving in the temple as priests. Nehemiah wants to know who's qualified to lead spiritually.

Pray

❷ *In your church, how do you celebrate and honour the finished work of Christ?*

❷ *What setbacks or problems do you see?*

❷ *How committed are your members?*

Pray for your church in the light of these questions.

Rebuilt by the word

*The people of Israel have finished working on the wall. Now God wants to more effectively work on **them**.*

Read Nehemiah 8:1-6

❷ *Who gathers to listen to God's word (v 1-3)?*
❷ *How long do they listen for (v 3)?*
❷ *What's their attitude towards God's word? Which phrases tell you this?*

⌄ Apply

❷ *What kind of thing makes you act the way the people do in verse 6?*
❷ *Do you respond that way to God's word? Why, or why not?*

Giving the sense

Read Nehemiah 8:7-12

Next, God's word is read again—but there is a difference this time. The people have heard the word. They have responded with emotion and passion. Now they are going to let it penetrate their lives.

❷ *What happens in verses 7-8?*
❷ *What's the people's immediate response (v 9)?*

The people's tears of joy turn into tears of conviction. They recognize that there is a distance between the way they are living and their commitment to the word of God.

❷ *But what do the leaders say (v 9-10)?*

The people are in a state of repentance. If you're repenting without sensing forgiveness, you're going to despair. But when you know you have forgiveness, you can worship and have satisfaction in the living King. This is what Nehemiah, Ezra and the other leaders want the people to do.

"The joy of the LORD is your strength" (v 10) means that you're hiding in something that's bigger than you. You are satisfied with the one who can cover you and take care of you. You're satisfied with the one who has forgiven your sin.

The people mourn and weep as they hear the word of the Lord, because they suddenly realize how much they need healing. But even as they start to cry out to God for help, they find that he has helped them.

⌃ Pray

Read Exodus 20:1-17 and Matthew 22:36-40. Reflect on each commandment and ask God to show you ways in which you have failed to keep his law. Confess your sin. Then rejoice! Praise God for the forgiveness that is found in Jesus.

⌄ Apply

It's important that this interaction with God's word happens in community.

❷ *On Sunday, how could you help those around you to listen to God's word carefully, understand it, and respond with worship, repentance, and joy?*

Bible in a year: Jeremiah 46 – 47 • Matthew 28 ✔

Building booths

Tears of contrition and shouts of joy have both followed the reading of God's word among his newly gathered people in Jerusalem.

On the second day, the leaders say to each other, *That's not going to catch us off guard again.* They gather for a little seminary class just by themselves.

Read Nehemiah 8:13-18

❓ *What does verse 13 tell us about who is gathering and why?*
❓ *What do they learn (v 14-15)?*

A way to remember

Leviticus 23 contains the instructions about this Feast of Booths or Tabernacles, which God gave to his people hundreds of years before Nehemiah. There were various aspects of this festival, but the key one for our purposes is in Leviticus 23:42-43.

Read Leviticus 23:42-43

❓ *What historical event was the booth-making supposed to remind people of?*
❓ *What would it have reminded them of about God?*

God was reminding his people of their birth as a nation—who he was, and who they were. He also wanted his people not to forget what it was like when times were hard. Remembering the days of hardship in the wilderness would mean that, when they arrived in the promised land, they would bless God for all he had provided. They would remember that he was the source of everything.

❓ *Why is this particularly relevant to the people of Nehemiah's time?*

It's deeply relevant to our own times, too. This passage is a call to us all to remember God's faithfulness.

The further away we get from remembering what God delivered us from, the more we develop a sense of entitlement—becoming thankless towards the goodness of God and believing that the good in our lives is deserved.

Nowhere is this more important than when it comes to the gospel of salvation. We have to know what it took to save us. We have to know that the God of holiness and wrath was rightly angered by our sin, so that when we get saved, we know that we weren't entitled to salvation but that it has come to us only because of the goodness and mercy of God (Ephesians 2:8-9).

A feast renewed

❓ *Who celebrates the festival and how (Nehemiah 8:16-18)?*

🔼 Pray

Reflect on all the undeserved blessings in your life. Praise God for them and ask him for his help in remembering his faithfulness and not taking him for granted.

Sackcloth and praise

After the celebration of Nehemiah 8, the people assemble again. This time, they are grieving.

Chapter 9 contains an overview of the redemptive record of God in the lives of his people. We see some beautiful things about how God has always been intervening and helping his people.

So why do they grieve? Because before you can appreciate who God is, you have to know who you're not. This is a moment of collective repentance.

Read Nehemiah 9:1-16

❷ *How do the people demonstrate their sense of humility before God and their discomfort about their sin (v 1)?*

They separate themselves from foreigners. This is because they are gathering in order to confess "their sins and the sins of their ancestors". In other words, they are saying to the non-Jews, *These are not your sins to be dealt with. These are our sins.*

❷ *What do they do before they confess (v 3)?*

As the reading went on, the people would have seen the gaps and absences in their lives in comparison to what God had commanded.

The Levites stand up to lead the people in prayer (v 4-5). But they don't start with confession. They start by praising God.

The Lord alone

❷ *What reasons are there to praise God in verse 6?*

❷ *How is God described in verses 7-8 and why?*

In Genesis 15 God made an unconditional covenant with Abraham. He promised to give him as many offspring as the stars. He promised that Abraham—or his offspring— would possess the land that he had been called to live in.

Nehemiah 9:9-15 describes some of the events of the book of Exodus.

❷ *How does the exodus story link to the story of Abraham (v 8, 15)?*
❷ *What evidence of God's power do we see in verses 9-15?*
❷ *What evidence of his faithfulness do we see?*
❷ *What other words would you use to describe God here?*

God was incredibly kind to Abraham's descendants. But, as verse 16 reveals (and as we'll see in more detail in the next study), they did not do much to deserve it.

⌃ Pray

Make verses 5-6 as your own prayer. Then make a list of as many examples of God's power and faithfulness that you can think of. Spend time praising him—and be honest with him about where you have failed to live up to what he is like.

Faithful and unfaithful

Nehemiah 9 is like an amazing love story—but it's mostly one-sided.

Read Nehemiah 9:16-38

The Levites now start to recount the unfaithfulness of their ancestors.

❷ *God rescued his people from Egypt. But how did they respond (v 16-18)?*

Acting presumptuously means having a sense of entitlement. These people thought God owed them something, no matter what they did. When we think that, we're in trouble!

❷ *What had the people forgotten (v 17)?*
❷ *Yet how did God respond, and why (v 17, 19-21)?*

The Levites don't stop with the exodus generation. Next they move on to the generations that lived in the promised land.

❷ *How do we see God's faithfulness in verses 22-25?*
❷ *How did the people respond (v 26)?*

As a result of their disobedience, the people were handed over to their enemies, experiencing oppression and domination by other nations (v 27). Yet when they repented and turned back to the Lord, he responded in mercy and provided deliverers (v 28).

❷ *In verses 27-31, how do the Levites prove that their description of God in verse 17 is true?*

God did not just provide for his people materially. He was ready to forgive. He was willing to continue the relationship with them despite past wrongs.

God is slow to anger. All of his people sin against him regularly, yet he puts his anger in neutral. He does it, of course, through Christ, who fully paid for the sin of all who trust in him.

Now therefore

Verse 32 highlights God's character yet again. The Levites know his integrity is perfect. It's on this basis that they make their request.

❷ *What do they ask (v 32)?*
❷ *What's their current situation (v 36-37)?*
❷ *Why (v 33-35)?*

The people are now going to make a covenant with God (v 38): a binding promise to be faithful to him.

❷ *Why do you think what they've said so far motivates them to do this?*

☑ Apply

❷ *Look back through the passage. Is there anything that God's people did that you, too, are guilty of in some way?*
❷ *How do the Levites' words about God's character encourage you?*
❷ *What commitment do you need to make to God today?*

From despair to where?

You may have read this psalm many times; or sung parts of it in church; or learned verse 8 by heart. It's a mind-blowing meditation on the experience of being forgiven.

Fantastic forgiveness
Read Psalm 32:1-2

❷ *What three kinds of sin does David mention here (in v 2 "sin" = "iniquity", ESV)?*
❷ *What is the difference between them, do you think (if any)?*
❷ *What is the spiritual deceit mentioned in v 2? Why is this important?*

David uses three words which describe different kinds of sin: *transgressions*—deliberate rebellion against God's will; *sins*—specific wrong thoughts, words or deeds; *sin/iniquity*—inner moral corruption. It's easy for us to lump all of our wrongs together under a general banner of "sin", glossing over the fact that we've wronged God in so many ways.

Yet, says David, this thoroughly rotten creature is blessed! The Lord does not count his wrongs against him! Only those who are honest with God (v 2) can be forgiven. As the Lord Jesus puts it in the Beatitudes, it is the poor in heart who are forgiven—those who know their own failure, and so look to Christ for forgiveness.

Conscious confession
Read Psalm 32:3-5

❷ *What is the journey that David goes on?*
❷ *When was the last time you felt your own sin so profoundly?*

Prayer and protection
Read Psalm 32:6-11

❷ *What will inevitably flow from a blessed and forgiven life (v 6, 7, 11)?*
❷ *What are the warnings that we should continue to be aware of (v 9)?*

David speaks wonderfully about being surrounded by people celebrating God's great acts of deliverance (v 7). And it just gets better. God promises to keep a watchful eye on his children (v 8). He promises to teach and instruct us how to live for him. But our response shouldn't be the forced obedience of a dumb animal (v 9), but rather the loving obedience of a son or daughter.

☑ Apply

❷ *We can get so used to being forgiven that we start to take it for granted. Do you understand how truly blessed you are to be forgiven?*
❷ *How often do you hear your own voice celebrating God's faithfulness?*

☒ Pray

Read through the psalm again, verse by verse, identifying David's experience with your own, and praising the Lord for his faithfulness.

Sacrificial commitment

Nehemiah 10 sees the people make a major recommitment to God.

In many ways this is Israel being re-established as a covenant nation, even though they are still under Persian occupation.

Read Nehemiah 10:1, 28-39

❷ *Who is making this commitment (v 28-29)?*

They "bind themselves with a curse and an oath". In other words, they say something like this: *I swear that I will walk according to God's law. And if I don't, let me be cursed.* They take it for granted that breaking God's covenant would incur punishment.

It's different for us today because Jesus cancels out the curses (Galatians 3:13). Now, when we sin, no curse comes upon us. The curse came upon him on the cross. However, we still need to hold ourselves accountable to our covenant with God, as the people in Nehemiah did. It may be helpful to think of a few people you trust and admire, people who are maturing in their faith, and give them permission to keep you accountable—rebuking you if you need it.

The commitments

Nehemiah 10:30-39 outlines the commitments the people of God are making for themselves. Essentially, they promise to keep God's law. Submission to the authority of God's word is the unmistakable principle at work.

❷ *What do they promise…*
- *v 29?*   • *v 30?*
- *v 31?*

❷ *How does each of these show submission to God?*

Next, they make financial commitments to the work of God in the temple (v 32-33).

❷ *What are they paying for (v 33)?*

They also promise various offerings. They will give God the first of their crops each year (v 35, 37), and dedicate their firstborn sons (v 36—see Exodus 13:11-15). Finally, they promise tithes (ten percent of their income).

❷ *How do they sum up what they're doing (v 39)? How does this show submission to God?*

✓ Apply

Our equivalent of paying for temple resources is giving money to the church to make sure that the sacrifice of Jesus is proclaimed.

❷ *Do you give regularly to the work of your church? If not, what could you give?*

But this passage also makes a wider point about our commitment to the Lord.

❷ *What would it look like in your life to fully commit your relationships, your work and rest, and your money to God?*
❷ *What practical steps could you take to make this commitment a reality?*

The joy of Jerusalem

It's time to get the city properly in order. Everyone has their place.

....

Read Nehemiah 11:1-6

Jerusalem is a wreck—ruined. Nobody wants to live there. And not everybody can fit anyway. So they cast lots. They put everyone's names in a hat and draw some out.

❓ *Why do you think the people bless those who offer to live in Jerusalem (v 2)?*

The people that settled in Jerusalem didn't just include those who were dedicated to temple service. Some of these lived out in the villages (v 3), while some of the other people lived in Jerusalem (v 4-6). There's no separation between professional religious workers and the rest of society.

Order and organisation

Nehemiah lists all the people who lived in Jerusalem (v 4-24). It's a reminder that these were real people—real individuals. Each person has his or her own place in God's plan.

Then he lists the different regions with each of their villages (v 25-36). They've taken possession of the whole of Judah—all the land that was once ruled over by the kings of Judah, from Beersheba in the south to the valley of Hinnom in the north (v 30). At last, the people are where they should be.

❓ *Given what we learned in Nehemiah 9 about the history of God's people, why is this so significant?*

The next thing Nehemiah puts in order

is the ministry leadership (12:1-26). We're given the names of the priests and leaders of the people across six generations.

The setting up of the priesthood and its legacy meant that the people would keep being helped to look Godward. That was how they would prevent further judgment and experience healthy fellowship with the Lord as a community. At least, that was the hope!

Dedicating the wall
Read Nehemiah 12:27-43

❓ *Why do the people gather again (v 27)?*
❓ *Where do the two choirs go (v 31, 37, 38-40)?*
❓ *What does the celebration feel like (v 43)?*

The walls were broken, the nation was broken, but now all that has changed. Jerusalem is the city of God again.

✔ Apply

❓ *In what ways do you see order in the world God has created?*
❓ *What particular place, roles and responsibilities has he given you? How can you make sure you do those well?*
❓ *Who has he put in leadership over you (especially in your church)? How can you honour that leadership?*
❓ *In what ways could you lead others in celebration of God this week?*

....

Uncompromised?

As the choirs sing in Jerusalem, we witness a wholehearted commitment to God's rule—or at least, what looks like it…

Read Nehemiah 12:44 – 13:3

It's still the day when the choirs sang in Jerusalem (v 44).

Willing to serve

❷ *Who is appointed in verse 44, and why?*
❷ *What is done in verse 45, and why (v 45-46)?*

The worship motivates the people. They're rejoicing and they want that joy to continue. They already promised to give tithes and contributions back in 10:32-39, but now they are figuring out how to actually make that happen (12:47).

⌄ Apply

The meticulousness we see here should apply to everything we do for the Lord.

The willingness of the people to serve and to give is also a challenge for us today. Everyone should be actively involved in some way.

Right away

❷ *What else happens on this same day (13:1-3)?*

Ammonites and Moabites had a long history of opposing God's people (see Numbers 22 – 24). This removal of foreigners should not be viewed as racial exclusivism. As always, foreigners could become part of Israel by conversion (Ezra 6:21; Ruth 1:16-17). God was concerned about spiritual influence. He wanted his people to have families that would pass on a commitment to himself—the kind of commitment we see in the people's swift actions in Nehemiah 13:3.

The bubble bursts

But before all of this happened, we are told, something else took place.

Read Nehemiah 13:4-9

The people's contributions were stored in a chamber in the temple. A man named Eliashib was in charge of it.

❷ *But what does he do (v 4-5)?*

Look back at 2:10, 19; 4:3, 7; 6:1-7, 12-13 to remind yourself of what Tobiah is like. This is the man Eliashib has given a foothold right in the centre of the community—and even inside the temple, which represented God's dwelling place.

❷ *How does Nehemiah deal with this (13:7-9)?*

⌄ Apply

Reading about Tobiah should prompt us to ask ourselves: what things in my life are out of order? Maybe it's your relationships, finances, or spiritual life. We must challenge the enemy and get things back under God's divine order. We must throw Tobiah out.

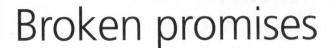
Broken promises

Tobiah's temple apartment is not the only problem Nehemiah encounters when he gets back to Jerusalem after some time away.

In fact, the people have compromised on all the commitments they made in chapter 10.

Read Nehemiah 13:10-31

❓ *What's the problem concerning tithes (v 10)?*
❓ *Why is this such a big problem (v 11)?*
❓ *How does Nehemiah sort it out (v 11-14)?*

Trustworthy (v 13) is a weighty biblical requirement. If a person is committed to the local church, that is weighty. If a person is committed to a spouse, if we raise our children in the fear of the Lord, if we go to work on time, if we pay our bills when they're due, it is significant. It is living the way God wants us to live. It is being like God, who is always faithful.

❓ *What is the problem in verses 15-16?*
❓ *Why does Nehemiah say it is so serious (v 17-18)?*
❓ *How does he deal with it (v 19-22)?*

Rest is not just a meaningless command—it is for our good. It is a vital discipline that keeps us centred on God in all of life. It is serious that the people have broken this promise, and that's why Nehemiah acts so decisively.

❓ *What promise has been broken in verse 23?*

It's a big deal that these children speak the language of the peoples around them instead of the language of God's people.

They have a deeper connection to the people of pagan cultures than to the people of God. And they can't understand the Scriptures.

This gets Nehemiah even more angry than he has been already— not with the children or the foreign wives but with the Jewish men who have broken their oath.

The Bible doesn't seem to judge the response of Nehemiah as good or bad (though I wouldn't recommend doing this today!). The focus is more on the importance of turning back to covenantal faithfulness.

❓ *What does Nehemiah fear (v 26-27)?*

Compromising God's word for the sake of personal preferences is a huge, huge mistake.

The one to please

Re-read Nehemiah 13:14, 22, 31

❓ *What do these verses tell you about Nehemiah's motives and priorities?*

⌃ Pray

God calls us to be a people of uncompromised faith. We need to live a life that's uncompromised and committed wholeheartedly to the Lord Jesus Christ.

Pray now for your heart and for the hearts of others in your church. Ask God to make you more and more faithful and to help you build his kingdom, to his glory.

NEHEMIAH FOR YOU

For Reading, for Feeding, for Leading

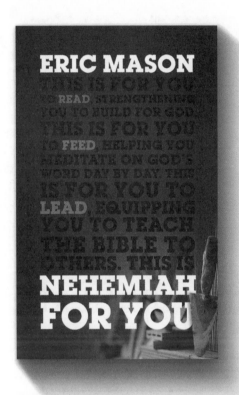

The book of Nehemiah chronicles a key moment in the history of God's people: the rebuilding of the walls of Jerusalem after the return from exile. But we don't walk away from this book just knowing about a rebuilt wall. Nehemiah helps us think through any type of rebuilding we might do for God—from our homes and families to our local church, our communities and our world. It teaches us about gospel mission.

Urban pastor Dr. Eric Mason unpacks this rich book verse by verse. He explains the context, gives plenty of application for our lives today, and shows us what it looks like to get involved in God's work to build his kingdom.

thegoodbook.co.uk/nehemiah-for-you
thegoodbook.com/nehemiah-for-you

Introduce a friend to

explore

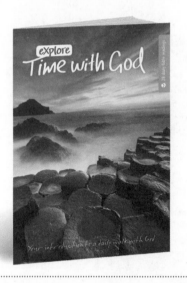

If you're enjoying using *Explore*, why not introduce a friend? *Time with God* is our introduction to daily Bible reading and is a great way to get started with a regular time with God. It includes 28 daily readings along with articles, advice and practical tips on how to apply what the passage teaches.

Why not order a copy for someone you would like to encourage?

Coming up next…

- ❥ 1 Kings
  with James Hughes

- ❥ Jonah
  with Nathan Buttery

- ❥ Luke
  with Jon Gemmell

- ❥ Micah
  with Frank Price

- ❥ Psalms
  with Jeremy Leffler

 Don't miss your copy. Contact your local Christian bookshop or church agent, or visit:

UK & Europe: thegoodbook.co.uk
info@thegoodbook.co.uk
Tel: 0333 123 0880

North America: thegoodbook.com
info@thegoodbook.com
Tel: 866 244 2165

Australia: thegoodbook.com.au
info@thegoodbook.com.au
Tel: (02) 9564 3555

India: thegoodbook.co.in
info@thegoodbook.co.in